Myths and Mortals

Myths and Mortals

FAMILY BUSINESS LEADERSHIP
AND SUCCESSION PLANNING

Andrew Keyt

WILEY

Published by John Wiley & Sons, Inc., Hoboken, New Jersey.
Published simultaneously in Canada.

For general information on our other products and services or for technical support, please contact our Customer Care Department within the United States at (800) 762-2974, outside the United States at (317) 572-3993 or fax (317) 572-4002.

Wiley publishes in a variety of print and electronic formats and by print-on-demand. Some material included with standard print versions of this book may not be included in e-books or in print-on-demand. If this book refers to media such as a CD or DVD that is not included in the version you purchased, you may download this material at http://booksupport.wiley.com. For more information about Wiley products, visit www.wiley.com.

Library of Congress Cataloging-in-Publication Data:

Keyt, Andrew, 1969–
  Myths and mortals : family business leadership and succession planning / Andrew Keyt.
    pages cm
  Includes index.
   ISBN 978-1-118-92896-7 (hardback) - ISBN 978-1-118-93229-2 (epdf) -
   ISBN 978-1-118-93230-8 (epub)
  1. Family-owned business enterprises—Succession. 2. Family-owned business enterprises—Management. I. Title.
   HD62.25.K49 2015
   658.4'092—dc23

                                                                        2015007884

Cover Design: Wiley
Cover Image: Monument ©iStock.com/Djete;
Circle Paving ©iStock.com/daizuoxin;
Walkway ©iStock.com/STILLFX;
Young Man ©iStock.com/Alija

Printed in the United States of America

10 9 8 7 6 5 4 3 2

To all of the graduates of the Loyola University Chicago's Quinlan School of Business Next Generation Leadership Institute. Your willingness to take on challenges, dream big dreams for both your families and businesses, and step into authentic leadership is the inspiration for this book.

And

To my parents, Marcia and Douglas Keyt, who gave me the foundation to find my own path, a path true to who I am

Contents

Preface   xi

Acknowledgments   xv

Prologue: Born in the Shadows

Grappling with the humanity of the hero   xix

Born in the Shadows   xx

Definition of the Myth   xxii

A Journey to Generative Leadership   xxii

I Am Not My Father (Differentiation)   xxvi

It Takes a Personal Vision   xxvii

Moving the Past into the Future   xxviii

Chapter 1   **Making of a Myth**

How stories of heroism help and harm a successor   1

The Power of the Myth   2

The Good Story   3

The Bad Story   4

Understanding the Reality of the Myth   6

Origins of the Myth   7

Feeding the Myth   8

If It Makes You Happy   9

Keeping the Next Generation in the Shadows   11

Idealization of the Child   11

Parentification of the Child   13

Infantalization of the Successor   13

Idealization's Alter-Ego   14

Reality and True Truth   16

Chapter 2   **Out of the Shadows**
The journey of the successor to lead apart from the myth   19
Differentiation and the Life Cycle   22
  Attending (0 to 18 months)   23
  Power (18 to 36 Months)   23
  Responsibility and Conscience (36 months to 5 years)   23
  Competency and Latency (5 or 6 to 11 years)   24
  Separation and Adolescence (12 to 23 years)   24
  Early Adulthood (20s and 30s)   24
Overcoming the Successor's Curse   25
From Hero to Human: Deconstructing the Myth of the Founder   27
When Successors Chart Their Own Course   31
When Idealization Interferes   32
Shining the Light Inward   33
Asserting the Self in the Family Legacy   37

Chapter 3   **You Gotta Earn It**
Earning your way to the top   41
Your Own Way   43
Be Honest with Yourself   44
  I Go Blind   46
  How Parents Can Help   47
  Building Belief in Others   48
Building Resiliency   49
Show Up for Work   52

Chapter 4   **The Strength of Failure**
Running the obstacle course of success   57
Developing Gut Instincts: Learning through Action   60
The Hard Road to Leadership   61
No Mistakes; Just Learning   62
Supporting Failure   65
Obstacle Courses   68
The Family Launching Pad: Go Out and Get It   69
The Shape of Success   69

Chapter 5   **"I Can See Clearly Now"**
The origins of a fresh vision for the family business   73
A Story for the Future: Mission, Vision, and Values   75

Respect the Past; Do What's Right for the Future   76

The Rudder of Conviction   78

Working through Personal Values   80

Family Planning   81

Mission   83

Back to the Future   84

Chapter 6   **Nonstop Learning**

Know your weakness and improve   89

Sustaining Credibility   91

Respectfully Pushing the Limits   93

Defining Success: Future Forward   94

Know Thy Motives   95

The Necessity of Continual Development   97

Disciple of the Disciplines   98

Staying Power   100

Chapter 7   **Feed the Family**

Caring for relationships, caring for the business   103

Dare to Be Different   105

Heart and Soul   107

Family Assets   110

How Competition Can Cripple   113

From the Founder to the Family   114

Next Generation   117

Chapter 8   **Me versus We**

Sharing the glory of the family business story   121

The "I" in the "We"   123

From Legendary to Ordinary   125

When the Magnetic Center Is Gone   126

Feels Like Family   127

More than Money   130

Dream Weaver   132

The Brick Wall   132

Re-Generation   133

Chapter 9   **Decisions, Decisions**

Decisiveness amidst ambiguity   135

The Great Differentiator   138

Cutting the Gordian Knot   139
One Decision after Another   141
Failure Makes the Business Hero   142
Trap of Perfectionism   143
Think and Do: The Decision-Making Process   145
Must-Have Courage   145
A Sense of Where You Are   147
Reorientation   148
The Orientation-Locked Family   149
A Decisive Workforce   150
Willing to Fail   151

Chapter 10   **The Inner Light**
A plan to illuminate a successor's path   153
The Need for a Personal Strategic Plan   154
A Plan to Differentiate   156
True North   158
Values   159
Mission   160
Action Plan   161
A Flexible Plan   162
Let There Be Love   163
Let There Be Light   164

Epilogue: Stepping out of the Shadows and into the Light of Your Leadership   167
Identifying the Myths   167
Self   168
Building Internal Credibility   169
Building External Credibility   170

Appendix A   Research Note   173

Appendix B   A Generative Retreat: 1/3 Activity (Body), 1/3 Reflection (Self),
1/3 Planning (Future)   175

About the Author   177
Index   179

Preface

It was the early 1990s. I was a fresh college graduate. Like many fresh-outs, I wasn't sure what to do with my life. I was passionate about people but didn't know how to turn that into a career. Becoming a psychologist was an option, but the life of a therapist was unappealing.

I felt very lost.

In my quest to match my passion with a career, I returned to my roots. My grandfather was a county judge in Ohio; my father was an attorney for Northern Trust in Chicago; my brother, a paralegal, was on track to become a lawyer. So what was my natural conclusion? Pursue law. I tested out the idea as a paralegal.

While working as a paralegal, I traveled to San Francisco to meet with a client. It was April of 1992. I remember it clearly. While I wasn't particularly enthralled with the work, I felt important as a 22-year-old flying cross-country to hobnob with attorneys and business people from a large multinational corporation. One night, while I sat in my hotel room at the Hyatt Embarcadero, the phone rang. It was my father. I knew something was wrong. My father never called. Normally, my mother called and handed the phone to my father: "Here, talk to your son."

My father (age 52), who had quit smoking 15 years before, said he had lung cancer.

I was shocked. Then I, along with my mother and two brothers (I am the middle child), rallied around the idea that it could be treated. My father would beat the cancer.

Slowly, it became clear that he would not. The weekend of July 4th 1992, my father was determined to get up to our summer home in Wisconsin for our annual family vacation. Because he was undeterred, we flew him up from Chicago. It was a short-lived and frightening vacation. He was hospitalized and then Medivacced to Chicago. For the next month, our family life was organized around getting our work done as quickly as possible, so we could spend as much time as possible with him at the hospital.

One month later, on August 6, my father asked me to stay a little later during my visit. My brothers and mother had left. Something weighed on him. He had some requests. His final one was to tell me that he was passing 100 percent of his ownership in the family business (a family farm) to me and not splitting it among me and my brothers.

I was incredulous: "We have a family business?" My father had spent much of his life insulating us from the pressures and challenges of working with family. He hadn't told us anything about the farm that he co-owned with his brother and cousins. Surprised with this revelation, I left the hospital, my head spinning with a list of things to do to help my dad.

That was the night he died.

On August 7, 1992, I woke up, a newly minted family business owner. While dealing with the grief of losing my father, I also grappled with the new challenge of understanding the family business. Although his one-sixth ownership wasn't Walmart money, it came with a set of expectations and responsibilities that I wasn't fully prepared for at the tender age of 22.

My father was the one to whom all of the cousins looked for input and advice. He was the one whom they trusted to make the right decisions. Now, they started to look to me to play the same role. But I was not my father. I had a psychology and music background; he was a tax attorney. I wondered how I could possibly take on this role.

Feeding the self-doubt were questions about why my father picked me and not one of my brothers. Most people, as I did, thought that my older brother, Bryan, would be the logical choice. He was the oldest and on the path to becoming an attorney. For whatever reason, my father chose me.

This was the beginning of my path to and passion for family business. Five years later, after pursuing additional education at Northwestern University, I landed at the Loyola University Chicago Family Business Center. Here, I was first exposed to the challenges of family business successors through the Next Generation Leadership Institute—an 18-month leadership development course specifically designed to help successors in a family business become the best leader that they can be—not the leader that their parents want them to be, but a leader that is true to him- or herself. A leader that leads with authenticity.

Leading this program for the last 18 years while helping it to grow and evolve, as well as witnessing the transformations in the leaders going through the program, inspired me to write this book. I am passionate about helping the world to not stereotype the family business successor as an unqualified, lazy person who got the job only because of his or her last name. I want the world to understand that the vast majority of successors are qualified; they work hard; and they only want success for their families and the people whom their business supports.

The world needs to understand the challenge that successors face in finding their own voice and establishing credibility with themselves and with others.

The stories of the successors in this book show a commitment to excellence, not entitlement; they reveal the humanity of having to grow up in the shadow of parents, grandparents, and others whom the world celebrates and mythologizes as all-powerful leaders.

We all face this challenge in some form: whether choosing *our* career versus those of our parents; taking the place of a mentor who helped shape who we are; or trying to repeat our parents' success as an actor, athlete, politician, or businessperson. The challenge is how to become one's own person in the shadow of those who have gone before.

We are all born into a story already being told. We are all, to some extent, following in the footsteps of those who went before us. At its heart, this book is about how one develops a unique sense of his or her identity without losing the connection to the family and what has gone before.

Although this book is written for the family business successor and his or her family, I hope that every reader can relate to the challenge of having to establish his or her sense of identity, credibility, and confidence in a world that wants to celebrate the past at the expense of creating the future.

Acknowledgments

As with any major endeavor, this book would not have happened without the love and support of my family and friends. I wrote this book with the help of many colleagues and friends. The ideas for this book have been shaped over a long period of time by those who have believed in me, taught me, and shared with me.

I'd like to start by thanking my brothers, Bryan and David, for their unwavering support in good times and in bad, and their wives, Debbie and Jenny, for always offering encouragement and feedback in the process. I'd like to thank my nieces and nephews—Bridget, Charlotte, Nathan, Owen, and Brandon—for reminding me to find joy in each day. I'd also like to thank Aunt Martha for her love and support.

In many ways, this book has been a personal journey, and it wouldn't have happened without my great friend and colleague Dr. Joe Astrachan. Early on in my career, Joe saw things in me that I didn't see in myself. He helped me to find my own voice in the field of family business. Much of my thinking about family business has been shaped and influenced by learning from and working with Joe. Joe helped me to conceptualize and shape this book, and it wouldn't have happened without him. Thank you, also, to his beautiful wife, Claudia, for her support.

Thank you to my friend and colleague Dr. Edward Monte for generously sharing his time in reviewing and commenting on the manuscript. Thank you to Dr. Robert Moore for teaching me so much about the process of identity formation.

Thank you to all of the successors who agreed to be interviewed for this book. Your generosity in sharing your stories will help many other family business successors feel less alone, while giving them the courage to create their unique visions for their family businesses. Thank you to Bill Wrigley, Christie Hefner, John Tyson, Dick DeVos, John Burke, Massimo Ferragamo, Pierre Emmanuel Taittinger,

Karl-Erivan Haub, Dave Juday, Steve Thelen, Joe Perrino, Mike Hamra, Alexander & Bella Hoare, Mary Andringa, Bob Vermeer, Sam Schwab, Ron Autry, Steve Don, Lansing Crane, Milt Pinsky, Mike Medart, Steve Thelen, Kurt Bechthold, Kathleen Thurmond, and Jean Moran. Thank you also to those who wish to remain anonymous.

Many people helped me with obtaining interviews, preparing the interview transcriptions, sifting through them, coding them, and shaping the ideas that emerged from them into the book that stands before you today. Thank you to my friend Liz Zabloudoff for her unwavering support of this project. Thank you to Kathryn McCarthy for the introductions and for helping me get a new perspective on the field. Thank you to my good friend and colleague Dr. Torsten Pieper for helping me understand the research processes and protocols for coding and analyzing the interviews. Thank you to Dr. Corinna Lindow and Dr. Isa Botero for working diligently to sift through the interviews, code them, and help me identify themes. Thank you to Bobi Seredich of EQ Inspirations who has been a part of this project from the beginning and to my friend and attorney Domingo Such who is always looking out for my best interests. Thank you to Melissa Parks and David Goetz at CZ Strategy for helping me to shape these themes and ideas as well as my experience into what I hope will be a book that can help family business successors for a long time to come. And thank you to Jennifer Muntz, Julie Kelly and the team at Cave Henricks for helping to spread the valuable lessons shared by the successors in this book.

I'd also like to thank my family at Loyola University Chicago's Family Business Center at the Quinlan School of Business; my family business center team: Anne Smart, Ryan Sinon, and Erin Kuhn Krueger; the member families who have put their trust in me and shared their stories of both joy and pain, struggles and triumphs, and shared so much with me over the years; the graduates of our Next Generation Leadership Institute for sharing your struggles and achieving great things—it is your stories that inspire the writing of this book; Dean Kathy Getz and the faculty of the Quinlan School of Business, especially my colleague Al Gini for his input and advice on the process of writing a book; my colleagues Tom Zeller, Dow Scott, and Serhat Cicekoglu for their support and collaboration; and my colleagues Mary Nelson, Fraser Clark, Mark Hoffman, Gary Shunk, Linda Balkin, and Lisa Ryan. A special thanks to my colleague

Dr. Carol Wittmeyer for her energy and support and continually teaching me the importance of showing gratitude.

To my family at the Family Business Network International and Family Business Network North America. Thank you to the families of FBN and the management team for allowing me to be a part of your story and building the strongest global network of family business owners in the world. What I have learned from being a part of this network is part of every page in this book. Specifically, I'd like to thank Alexis Du Roy, Olivier de Richoufftz, and Julia Mart for their friendship and support.

To my clients from 20 years of consulting—thank you for trusting me to support, push, poke, and prod your families in hopes of finding new ways to communicate, new opportunities to build unity and connection, and new ways to build more successful families and businesses. I am honored by the trust that you place in me.

Thank you to those who helped me find the path of working with family businesses—Dr. John Ward, Ken Kaye, and John Messervey. And those scholars and colleagues who have taught and influenced me in the classroom, through collaboration with clients, or their writing: Dr. George Manners, Ernesto Poza, Fredda Herz Brown, Greg McCann, Katherine McCarthy, and James Hughes.

The challenge of stepping out of the shadows of those who have gone before is not easy. It takes strength, self-awareness, support, feedback, and failures. I have faced all of these in the writing of this book, and it would not have happened without the contributions of those mentioned here.

Prologue: Born in the Shadows

Grappling with the humanity of the hero

The hour was late in London. And jet lag was creeping in. Though exhausted—physically, mentally, and emotionally—Bill Wrigley Jr., son of William Wrigley, heir of the William Wrigley Jr. Company, founded by his great grandfather William Wrigley Jr., hammered out a business deal with his partners from India. At Bill's initiative, the company was exploring expansion into India. At the age of 28, Bill Jr. was spearheading this effort as well as running the Canadian subsidiary and chewing-gum base subsidiary, which supplied materials to all of the company's manufacturing facilities worldwide. He was traveling the world at a dizzying pace.

Bill had been named assistant to the president, but he already felt the impending weight of future leadership. Adding to the emotional load was the burden of trying to run his areas of responsibility just like his father did—trying to be everywhere at once and managing every detail. As he remembers it, "I was running around … trying to be like my dad." In the London flat that night, the pressure bore down on him. Bill Jr. withdrew momentarily from the meeting, not feeling well, and was sick in the bathroom. Returning to the meeting immediately after, he finished the business at hand. When the meeting was over, Bill thought to himself, "If I keep operating like this, I'm not going to make it to 40!"

His mind reeled as he thought back to recent events of the previous day, as well as the culmination of traversing three continents in a matter of days and overseeing the painstaking details he was managing as he followed his father's path. That night, Bill's gut told the truth: The stress of emulating his father was beginning to clash with who he was and who he wanted to be as a leader. This internal dissonance prompted him to give a voice to the truth: "From this point forward, I am going to start doing things differently."

Getting sick that night was a pivotal point in Bill's life. He steered away from his father's style of leadership and began defining what style of leadership resonated with Bill—the next generation. He made a break.

Bill realized that he was trying to emulate not just his father but also the command-and-control leadership philosophy of an entire generation of Americans. They were the Greatest Generation, leading in a way that worked for a country emerging from the Great Depression and World War II. And Bill's father exemplified the best of that generation: a strong work ethic, loyalty to his people, and genuine compassion for them. For years, the company had thrived under this leadership style.

But it wasn't working for Bill, for one increasingly obvious reason—a blind spot so big that Bill had initially lost himself in it: He was not his father, though he was trying to be him.

The involuntary gut check in London prompted an integrity check as well. Leading as his father led was frustrating and stifling to him, because it wasn't true to Bill's strengths and his skill sets as well as his personal philosophy of how to get the best out of people.

It also stifled the company. The command-and-control model, which Bill describes as "the pollinating bee effect," demanded that every decision, no matter how small, got the "king" bee's approval. "If you wanted to change the color of the carpet in China, the approval had to come from my father's desk!" In effect, the pollination was inhibiting growth. What had been so successful in the 1950s, 1960s, and 1970s now frustrated innovation among the organization's top leaders across the globe. Bill realized that he would have to redefine a vision of success for himself first, and then for the company.

Born in the Shadows

This scenario plays out in different ways for people like Bill, children of powerful parents who are called to lead successful family businesses into the next era. These children are born into a story already being told about their parents, their families, and businesses. Larger than life, the stories of heroism, history, and success seem impossible to replicate. Historically, family businesses have been the backbone of our economy and our communities, and the stories of the founder and the family have grown with each succession. Family businesses, however, are more than lore; they are the natural unit of our economic enterprise. They take greater ownership and responsibility for the long-term well-being of their businesses, through stewardship of both their financial assets and investing in their employees, and their communities.[1]

I believe that family businesses can continue to solidify our economies into the future. But the challenge is great. Huge corporations dominate the economic landscape. Many of these are relatively new, responsive organizations that started small but grew to rule the market (like Amazon and Google). We laud entrepreneurs who build these companies, and often overlook those who have built strong and stable organizations across generations. Building a strong business is one challenge; building an organization that can sustain both a family and a business that benefits family, employees, and the community across generations is an entirely different challenge.

The individuals at the center of these legacy companies are family business successors. These successors have the herculean task of trying to establish their own identities, passions, and beliefs, and develop their own leadership styles while dealing with the expectations and shadows of their parents', grandparents', and great grandparents' success.

My 20 years working with family business owners and teaching successors in the Next Generation Leadership Institute at Loyola University Chicago's Quinlan School of Business and through Next Generation activities with the Family Business Network confirms the struggle of a successor to emerge from the shadows cast by these stories. In one sense, the stories help successors make sense of their relationship with their parents and their family history. They can inspire the successor to think big. But too often in the telling of these stories, the parents' failures and vulnerabilities become appendices to the larger narrative, or are lost altogether in the repeated recounting of their heroics. If a parent is building an empire, a child reasons, the stories explain their parents' absence and why they always felt like a runner-up in the pick of priorities. The stories create myths of the predecessor, encouraging the idea that the successor must lead without vulnerability or failure, and that success comes from an almost magical quality that their parent possesses. This prompts the next

---

[1]D. Miller and I. LeBreton-Miller, *Managing for the Long Run* (Boston: Harvard Business School Press, 2005) p.18–31.

generation to excessively emulate their parents and to avoid failure at all costs. What confidence a successor may possess can be crushed by the monolithic message, "You'll never be as good as your dad."

Definition of the Myth

When these stories are treated as truth, they can have an inspiring effect on both the family and the business. But when the stories grow into legends, they can lose their grounding in facts. They become myth, an amalgamation of fact and fiction that can cast a very long shadow. When it conveys a worldview based on values of self-determination, caring for employees and the community, hard work, and achievement, a founding myth can be a powerful generative force in a family. But when a myth focuses exclusively on the founder or the family mythology (in later generation family businesses), it stifles the family and curtails the legacy. The shadow lengthens as the story is interpreted by family, employees, customers, and the community. Wanting to create a heroic leader, we overlook the weaknesses, failures, and idiosyncrasies that are also a part of the story. And wanting to bask in the glory of the myth, many predecessors encourage its growth and development. In the mythical version, the predecessors become like deities.

The shadow the mythology creates makes the successor's task seem almost impossible, and the predecessor's success seemingly magical. The truth shows otherwise. The successes of the predecessors and of the family were the result of hard work and vision, combined with failure, doubts, the contributions and support of others, and even a bit of luck. Too often, the ego enjoys bathing in the glory of this myth, encouraging it to flourish.

This book explores how next-generation leaders who follow in the footsteps of their mythic parents, grandparents, as well as aunts and uncles, can step outside of the shadows these stories create and leverage their legacy for success, see their parents in the light of reality, and understand their own gifts and bring them to the table for the benefit of both the family and the business.

A Journey to Generative Leadership

Over the course of several years, I have interviewed successors in family businesses from across the globe, children of iconic families who stepped out of the shadow of the myth. Such leaders include

Bill Wrigley Jr., Christie Hefner, Pierre Emmanuel Taittinger, Massimo Ferragamo, John Tyson, Dick DeVos, Karl-Erivan Haub, and many others. I have interviewed successors from second-generation to eleventh-generation family businesses—all of whom grew up in the shadow of highly successful parents (and sometimes grandparents and great-grandparents) and yet took their family business to another level of success. Amidst self-doubt, family scrutiny, employee skepticism, and public pressure, these leaders took on the difficult job of following either a founder or another successful ancestor, and established themselves as authentic, credible, and generative leaders. They figured out how to lead in a way that emerged from a strong sense of who they are. They did not merely copy the predecessor's leadership approach, "attaching" their personality to it. Instead, they learned to be guided by their own rudder of conviction and step into their unique talents, interests, and experiences.

Myths and Mortals is the story of how successors become strong leaders in their own right, demystifying the idealized version of their predecessors and recognizing their shortcomings as well as honoring their successes. These leaders step out of the shadows of their predecessors and define a new reality for themselves, their family, and their business. This book is not the definitive narrative of the stories of these well-known families and businesses, but it is the authentic narrative of these successors who have had the courage to step out of the shadows of their parents, step into leadership, and improve on what has been given to them. In my research, I discovered that while there were clear indicators that someone would succeed in the family business, each story was unique. That's because each person had to wrestle with the task of developing a realistic sense of the predecessor (their strengths and weaknesses) and who he or she was (his or her strengths or weaknesses). Massimo Ferragamo, second-generation member of Salvatore Ferragamo, explained it this way:

Some people chase [their parent's success] for their lifetime—sons of actors, sons of singers, they think that they can be just like them and always live with a cloud of [the] parent in their lives. This is very dangerous because everyone is different ... you have to understand what your calling in life [is], what you should be doing and improve on what has been given to you, but you can't emulate.

The chase to be like someone else is exhausting, unending, and unattainable. A son or daughter cannot catch up to that which he or she was never meant to be. In fact, based on my research, I discovered that successors who develop a strong sense of self-awareness, a sense of their own identity, who can separate themselves from their legendary parents and grandparents, have the greatest chance of creating what is most foundational to success in a family business—credibility. Credibility has two components: believing in yourself (internal credibility) and others believing in you (external credibility). It's having enough self-confidence to inspire others' confidence in you.

Internal credibility is the degree to which we perceive ourselves to be qualified, trustworthy, and capable in the world. Internal credibility starts when our parents give us an inherent sense that we are valued and loved for who we are. We then can measure our credibility by our performance at certain tasks and by external verification of success. Internal credibility is solidified when we hear someone else tell us, "You did a great job." This objective verification can reinforce a subjective understanding of ourselves as valuable. We have inherent value, but we also have value in the world.

External credibility is the degree to which we have established our reputation with others, who come to believe we are qualified, competent, and credible through our actions and behaviors. We establish external credibility objectively through our performance and our track record, and subjectively by our ability to understand and have empathy for others and respond appropriately to their needs. We know we have external credibility when people choose to follow us.

It's impossible for a successor to lead without credibility. The mere reality of being a successor encourages the successor to think about his value, strengths, and skill sets only in relation to his parents and grandparents. In many ways, a young leader in a family business is in the one-down position. Employees may think he or she doesn't truly deserve the role of leader. Board members may support the decision, but inwardly think, "She will never be like her father." And the media tend to look for news that supports failure, not success. This is the *successor's curse.*

This was the case for the Steinbrenner family, the owners of the New York Yankees. For years, George Steinbrenner (widely referred to as "The Boss") and the New York Yankees dominated the

New York City sports scene. New Yorkers revered Steinbrenner for bringing championship baseball back to the world's most dynamic city. In November 2008, due to declining health, George passed the reins of the Yankees to his son, Hal. In contrast to George's gregarious, publicity-hungry personality, Hal was introverted and preferred to focus on the business of baseball rather than seeking the spotlight. Stepping into the role that his father had filled for so long was a daunting task.

This stark contrast in personalities between father and son led many in the New York press to question Hal's passion for baseball, his commitment to winning, and his ability to lead baseball's most famous franchise. In fact, in 2014, four years after his father's death, and six years after he became the managing partner of the Yankees, *The New York Post* published an article titled "Hal Steinbrenner Reveals a Very Un-Boss-Like Agenda for Yankees." The shadow cast by George Steinbrenner's legacy continues to draw public focus to the ways Hal is different from his father, and the automatic assumption is that this is bad.[2] In referencing the Yankee's inability to make the playoffs in 2014, this article notes that George Steinbrenner's traditional approach was to assign blame and fire managers in an attempt to appease the fans. Yet Hal set a different course when he responded to the media. He said, "Changes will not be made in the organization for show. You will be held responsible if the job is not getting done. Any change we do make, I will feel the job was not getting done and we could do better."

The assumption is that in order to be successful, you have to lead the way of the predecessor. The reality is that Hal's skill sets may be better suited to the needs of today's Yankees, but this will be determined over time. First, Hal's task is to prove himself, to earn his credibility, and build his track record. Hal Steinbrenner faces the constant challenge of living in his legendary father's shadow, questioned at every turn when he does something that seems different from the way George would have done it.

This type of questioning can make successors feel like mere mortals in the shadow of their mythic parents. It can spur self-doubt, the biggest obstacle to their credibility and to becoming a generative leader, someone who can build a foundation for success across

---

[2]Joel Sherman, "Hal Steinbrenner Reveals a Very Un-Boss-Like Agenda for Yankees," *New York Post* (October 1, 2014).

generations. At some level, every leader has to believe in his or her right to lead. It's a long, tortuous road to establish credibility in a successful family business. But those who succeed have figured out a way to establish authenticity and, consequently, credibility, which serves as a foundation for successful leadership. One of the tasks in establishing this credibility is to become aware of—and then to address—the myths surrounding the success of the previous generation.

I Am Not My Father (Differentiation)

Successors can easily lose themselves when they are caught in the shadow of a dominating mythology. Family businesses (and the myths surrounding them) encourage enmeshment, the belief that everyone should think in one way. This stifles the individual's sense of autonomy and sense of personal boundaries. The process of finding one's self starts when the successor can begin to separate and push against the predecessor. Bill Wrigley Jr. started that separation when he realized, "I am not my father. I don't have to lead like him."

Separating is the process of differentiation, which is the cornerstone of a family business legacy's foundation, and a theme I will come back to repeatedly in this book. Differentiation is the ongoing work of developing a strong sense of self, and harnessing that strength for the growth of the family legacy. Everyone is faced with the task of differentiation, of growing up to become their own person. However, it's especially challenging for successors who bring family legends to work with them every day. The more dominant the mythology and the more powerful the personality that fuels it, the harder it becomes for a successor to downsize the hero and make him human, and to break free of the shadow.

Differentiation is a successor's inner work, and it is a lifetime process. My research shows that successful successors become generative leaders by developing a practice of pursuing differentiation and establishing a strong sense of self. Bill Wrigley pushed the William Wrigley Jr. Company to reinvent itself when he found the strength to push away from his father and lean into his own convictions. At that point, he realized he could do things differently from his father. Bill Wrigley released himself from his father's shadow so that he could focus his energies and his emotion on doing what he needed to do to sustain the family legacy. He moved from emotional inertia to action.

It Takes a Personal Vision

The work of differentiation leads to inner illumination, as the successor, no longer eclipsed by the shadow of a legendary founder, begins to find out who she is and what she wants. The inner light of knowing one's self shines outward and becomes the source for developing a personal vision.

To know one's self is to recognize the humanity of those leaders who led before, as well as the humanity of those within the family and the business. Generative successors perpetuate the family legacy as they understand that their legendary predecessors were mortals with a heroic stripe. Given their flaws, the heroism of founders and their predecessors is all the more remarkable.

Bill Wrigley reflected this understanding when he introduced the motto, "Respect the past, but always do what's right for the future." This was born out of his recognition that while many of the traits of his father's leadership were core to its success, they may not serve the company well moving forward. His father's drive and authority were why the company grew during an era following the great world wars.

But to lead the company into a rapidly changing global environment, Bill realized he would have to reengineer the organization, and "do what's right for the future." This is where values meet vision, and successors must craft their own personal vision for the future to carry family values forward, rather than merely emulating what their parents did.

Defining one's success, independent from the way parents, family, and the community define it, is critical in differentiated leadership. What distinguishes successful successors in family businesses is their ability to respect and understand the past, while charting their own path, even in the face of resistance. The strength for defining one's own success comes from the hard work of separation, stepping out of the shadows of the myth: "I am not who my parents or anyone else want me to be." The leader's vision is formed both by traits shared with his or her parents *and* traits foreign to them. Leaders who embrace both establish a unique identity. They achieve personal authenticity and political credibility, foundational to establishing a vision of success.

A personal vision is the door that swings between internal and external credibility.

Later in this book we will examine how successors establish confidence in themselves and credibility with others. My research will show that family business leaders who succeed differentiate by building self-awareness, building a belief in themselves, and building the belief in others that they can be credible and generative leaders. This process leads successors to develop a rudder of conviction based on a clear sense of passion and values. Vision then leverages this inner work and turns it outward to the world. Successors have paid their dues; vision pays it forward. Vision is more than how one sees the world. It is also how the world sees a person as he projects himself to the world.

True vision is the extension of one's true self, how leaders serve their core convictions, so others know what matters to them.

Strong leaders can pursue those convictions in the most unlikely of circumstances. Christie Hefner wanted to work on Capitol Hill, but she altered her career trajectory to work at Playboy Enterprises. As different as she was from her father, Hugh Hefner, Christie was able to lead Playboy alongside him. He was its personae, and she was its voice. "I wasn't interested in being a personality, or, God forbid, a celebrity," Christie says. "I had to chart my own course. As different as my father and I are, he is authentic and true to himself, and I needed to be authentic and true to myself." The hard work of establishing internal credibility converges into a personal vision of success that makes the business more successful in achieving its mission.

Moving the Past into the Future

If a successor fails to differentiate, the family business most often fails to move its legacy forward. A differentiated leader is able to cast a vision that others can rally around simply because it is a vision that she can take charge of. Guided by her own rudder of conviction as well as her unique talents, interests, and experiences, she casts a unique vision for the time in which she is called to lead. A compelling vision, including shared values, is a motivational force. Values make people stay; a vision gets them going; and the meaning generated motivates people to pursue a larger purpose. It ignites a community and changes its culture. This is what Bill Wrigley did at his family retreat in Lake Geneva with his global leadership team, shortly after his father's passing in 1999. Bill aspired to create a new culture that encouraged the behavior he was looking for from his leadership team and, by extension, all the employees of Wrigley. In doing so, he worked with his team to set the company on a new growth trajectory.

This became apparent the night he gathered 60 leaders from around the world to a company pow-wow. Every element of the meeting was a departure from the past. "We had everyone exercising at 7 a.m.," he says, "and eating foods they had never seen on a plate. We had a session on listening, another on developing healthy company gossip, and at the end of every evening—and keep in mind this was 10 o'clock at night—we passed around a talking stick and participants reflected on the day." One of the outcomes was a clearer recognition of how each member of the leadership was responding to the change. A *player* was fully engaged and exploding with energy, a *passenger* was curious but reluctant. The challenge was to turn the passenger into a player. The *prisoners* were the leaders who sat with their hands folded across their chests. These were "not the kind of people we wanted for the company we were building," says Bill Jr.

For the crowning moment of the Lake Geneva leadership summit, he took an old concept and gave it a new meaning. "I wanted to build a microcosm of how this company should work worldwide, and I wanted to do it without flying around the world, as my father had."

Bill told all 60 leaders to break out by their geographical regions and to discuss fresh ideas for the company. Earlier in the week, the entire group had compiled a list of things that were wrong with the company. "Wipe the slate clean of all that excess baggage," Bill said, "and take your ideas and go pollinate other groups with them."

In a simple exercise, Bill had democratized the pollination process.

What his dad had done solo, the corporate leadership was doing as a team. The hierarchy of command-and-control had become a hive of cooperation and cross-pollination. When the buzz subsided, an incredulous participant asked a question that harkened back to the old days: "Who's going to approve all these plans?"

Bill took a few moments to absorb the question, with all its implications. Then he replied, "This is our plan. They are all approved. Let's go out and get it done." The room erupted with cheers. A new era had begun at Wrigley

Just as the bout of nausea in a London flat had been a pivotal personal crisis for Bill, when his gut told him that he had to change, the Lake Geneva pollination session was a turning point for the entire Wrigley organization. "That night, some of the old guard decided to leave," Bill Jr. says.

And those who stayed followed him into the future.

1

Making of a Myth

How stories of heroism help and harm a successor

Hollywood Boulevard, the early 1920s. It was the Golden Age of Cinema. Starlets were fetching their dreams, and so was a young shoemaker from Italy.

A scrap from a scrapbook, the photograph reads like a chapter from an autobiography. A lady sits on a curvaceous mohair sofa, her foot propped on a stool. Salvatore Ferragamo stoops over in white overalls—"like an artist or painter," his son, Massimo, chairman of Ferragamo USA, recalls—sketching a shoe as he studies the size and curve of the lady's foot.

"In that picture is everything," Massimo says. "My father always said, 'Whenever a customer comes into the store, you should make them feel like a princess. And each time a princess walks into your store, you should make them feel like a queen.'" Salvatore Ferragamo crafted shoes for heirs of royalty, even those who knew no pedigree, title, or crown. It was his talent of interpreting peculiar and extravagant requests, like a shoe with ostrich feathers, matched by his heart for customers, that made him wildly popular.

Decades later, Marilyn Monroe sat on Ferragamo's sofa. She was beautiful but short. To be taller, she always wore four-and-a-half uncomfortable inches of heel. But Salvatore, who studied anatomy at the University of Southern California, made a shoe comfortable that she felt beautifully tall in. Massimo says this was typical of his father: "Everything he did throughout his life, he did with incredible heart and creativity."

Salvatore died when his youngest son, Massimo, was almost three years old. But even today, his father is ever-present: "Almost every day I find myself telling the story of my father," he says. "When one leaves a legacy like he left, it's indestructible."

The stories Massimo retells hint at the heroic. At 15, Salvatore Ferragamo boarded a ship to the States by himself, and briefly worked in a cowboy boot factory in Boston. Disenchanted with the one-size-fits-all assembly-line production of shoes, Salvatore headed west and opened a shoe repair and made-to-order shop in California. There his empire was born—and where he staked his claim as the "Shoemaker to the Stars." Thirteen years later, he returned to his homeland, expanding the business, then filing for bankruptcy during the Depression, and then rebuilding the business in the 1950s. When Salvatore passed away in 1960, hundreds of artisans produced hundreds of handmade shoes daily.

"Though there were setbacks," says Massimo, "he always recovered from them and always made [his family's] life better and helped everyone that was around him." One such story was that of an old man named Zacharia. When Salvatore's shoe business lost its footing, he was so poor he couldn't even pay for a ride home from work. Zacharia would take Salvatore home in his horse-drawn carriage. Every ride Salvatore would say, "I have no money, but one day I will repay you." When Zacharia died, Salvatore found Zacharia's wife, paid his debt, and hired their daughter to work in the factory.

Like many successors, Massimo's admiration of his father was fueled by the myth of his father: the testimony of family, friends, the community, employees, suppliers, buyers, and even scrapbook news clippings. Salvatore's rags-to-riches story was studded with kindness, perseverance, and dedication to a craft. "I always grew up with great admiration for what he did and for how he did it—for the sacrifices," says Massimo. "How lucky [am I] that I had a father who did things like that?" The stories of Salvatore's sacrifices not only connected Massimo to his deceased father, but they also transmitted the values core to the Ferragamo brand: integrity, value, craftsmanship, tradition, and timeless excellence.

The Power of the Myth

Heroic stories of visionary leaders—such as Salvatore Ferragamo, who take risks and do amazing things—can cast a long shadow.

Their accomplishments, challenges faced, and a long list of successes are monolithic and magical. These stories are powerful and map out a view of the world. They create a system of values and beliefs that shape the way that family, successors, and employees see themselves and the company. Their influence on the next generation is both positive and negative. Their legacy can either illuminate an exciting path for the next generation to follow into the future or cast a shadow that stifles the growth and development of the next generation. It is in the shadow that the myth of the heroic and invincible parent or family expands. Successors can follow down the rabbit hole of a myth or emerge from the shadows onto a new path of their own making. Every family has a mythology that has both generative and destructive power, which either builds or erodes the foundation for the future of the family business.

The Good Story

Stories can both help and hurt a successor's development. The myths and stories about Salvatore Ferragamo helped young Massimo connect to his father, who died when Massimo was almost three years old. These stories provided a foundation of values and principles to guide him, and a core belief that great things are possible. They helped to make meaning of what had gone before. This is the generative aspect of a mythology, and it is usually system-centric, meaning that it engages everyone in the family system towards establishing a foundation of clear values, a clear sense of purpose, and a vision for the future. It is not built to feed the ego of the individual or create an idealized image of the perfect family. Wanda Ferragamo ensured that her husband's vision was stronger than his legend, and she made sure that all her children traced their own paths within the family business to fulfill Salvatore's vision.

The stories of great family business leaders connect successors to the past and help to make sense of what has gone before. They provide a sense of stability and belonging, and often transmit the values that form the foundation for a successor's leadership success. I talked to a fourth-generation leader of a 100-year-old retail company. Founded in the late 1800s, the company manufactured clothing, and over the years established a broad network of retail stores across the Midwest. As the retail environment became increasingly challenging, the family shifted to become one of the strongest online retailers in their space. In 2009, a family that had survived two world wars, the Great Depression, and countless recessions was still at the top of its game. When I asked its 40-year-old leader how the company was surviving the economic downturn, he said, "We made it through the Depression, so we can make it through this."

Karl-Erivan Haub, CEO of the multibillion-dollar global retailer Tengelmann Group, talks of his family history, how his parents, grandparents, and great grandparents survived two world wars, five currency changes, and multiple economic crises. He says, "It creates the notion that, OK, these generations have suffered through that. They persevered and we have to persevere."

The stories of the successes of their parents, grandparents, and great-grandparents grounded these successors with the confidence that they would overcome almost any challenge that they would face. These stories foreshadowed an end to the story: Everything would be OK.

Mary Vermeer Andringa, Chairman and CEO of the Vermeer Corporation, an agricultural and industrial equipment manufacturer, recalls the values passed on through the stories of her father, Gary Vermeer. A pilot, her father often drew analogies to flying in speeches he delivered to staff and dealers. To calm people in the midst of a down market, he would talk about how between take-off and landing, weather can shift from clement to inclement or from inclement to clement. The point he made is one that the organization draws on to this day: "Things never get so good, like good weather, that they don't get worse; and things never get so bad, like bad weather, that they don't get better." At their best, the stories of family business predecessors are a guiding light for a successor on the journey to developing credibility as the next generation leader.

These myths are most helpful and productive when they transmit a sense of stability as well as a sense of values and culture that can help guide behavior. They provide a sense of meaning and purpose to a large and often complex system.

The Bad Story

But every myth has its dark side. The myth of a family business is destructive when it becomes egocentric, bolstering the ego of the founder or the collective ego of the family. All the energy of the myth is concentrated on making a hero of a leader rather than energizing the entire family across generations. It doesn't tap into the passions, beliefs, inspiration, and contribution of others in the family and the business. It is driven primarily by the need to promote the ego of one individual or protect the family image. The myth spins out stories that laud successes, while stripping away the faults, failures, and vulnerabilities that make these people and their families human. At their best, myths convey truth, but an egocentric mythology creates a feeling of inauthenticity instead. The system seeks to protect its image by pretending that the failures, problems, and vulnerabilities don't exist. They aggrandize the good and parse out the bad, focusing on heroics rather than incorporating failure into the narrative. In fact, an entire area of publishing memorializes this idea—that of *vanity press*. While not every book written about the founding or history of a family business has the *vanity* narrative, many do. These are books where larger-than-life leaders seek to legitimize and tell stories of their own greatness. While this feeds their egos and tells a great story, it can suck the air out of the room for a successor. It seems the legendary leader is responsible for all of this success.

This destructive mythology can create a shadow that eclipses the talent of future family leaders, who are unable to find their sense of identity and strength, to discover their passions, and to determine what beliefs they hold in common with parents and family, and where they differ. Caught in this shadow, successors can wilt and die. They often succumb to entitlement, addiction, depression, and unhappiness. When the successor gets caught in the shadow, these families tend to deteriorate into infighting, anger, self-protection, and selfishness. These families tend to produce successors with low self-esteem and self-worth. One-dimensional narratives of a fearless and visionary leader also establish the wrong idea that a successor must also lead without fear, doubt, or vulnerability. These stories encourage the belief that the successes of their predecessors were magical and repeating similar feats would be impossible. Successors wrongly conclude that in order to be successful, you have to be born with magical (and unattainable) leadership traits.

These myths can also create the idea—as it did for Bill Wrigley Jr., former CEO of the William Wrigley Jr. Company—that successors must lead in the way their father/mother led. When a child excessively emulates her parent, she thinks, "My father was a legend, so I must be just like him in order to lead the organization—or not lead at all." And others surrounding the family business, as in the Steinbrenner case, feed that narrative.

Understanding the Reality of the Myth

We are all born into a story already being told. In the context of a family business, these stories become larger than life and, often, become myths. These stories that we tell are not of one person's making, they are built on people's perceptions of what happened, and not what actually happened. They are often idealized interpretations expressed by many individuals: employees, the community, the press, as well as the parents and successors themselves. Simply, the stories don't tell the whole story. A founder may have led an organization through the Depression, like Salvatore Ferragamo—a heroic feat. A founder may have sold paper to Paul Revere to produce the first Continental Currency. The family may have personally sacrificed to avoid layoffs in the Depression. Or the family may have saved much of Fleet Street during the Nazi bombing of London. But these stories often distort reality by telling only one part of the story. They focus on the positive outcomes, often overlooking challenges and failures and vulnerabilities that led to the success. They combine the stories of many and tell it as if it were one. They create a story of mythic proportions that seems impossible to repeat.

To believe that the success of a parent magically exists apart from his (and often his family's) sacrifice, the ideas and support of others, good timing, hard work, and a lot or a little luck, is to live in the shadow of the myth. In retelling the stories, successors create a narrative that further shadows reality: "I can never be like her!" This is shadowland living: to live life in reaction to these stories of the past rather than creating possibilities (and stories) for the future.

The fact is, a predecessor's qualities and skill sets may not be the qualities and skill sets that the company will need in its leader to move forward. The faster its pace and the bigger it becomes, the more a business requires a different type of leader for it to thrive. The skills needed to start a business and build it to a $50 million company are very different than the skills needed to grow to a $100 million or $200 million company.

Mythologizing also can build up an individual while skimming over the truth that the successes were earned by the hard work of many and the good fortune accumulated over time. Myths don't account for learning that comes from repeated failure, the dogged persistence, and the small disciplines that form the backbone of greatness. Instead of tempering these myths and grounding them in reality, children can get caught up in their grandness, projecting their parents as mighty and all-powerful figures. Once that story has built momentum, it is hard to reel in reality. The predecessor keeps getting bigger while the successor shrinks into the shadows.

For a young leader to step out of this shadow, he or she must winnow truth from myth. It's part of the work that precedes success. Each family's mythology has a mix of generative qualities and destructive tendencies. It tells stories that teach values that inspire and unify families, as well as stories that stifle a family's creative energies. Show me a successful successor in a family business, and I'll show you someone who sorted through the myth, separated truth from fiction, and began to build on the past with a fresh approach to leadership. They become generative leaders by leveraging the legacy of their family and building a foundation to meet the needs of future generations. These successors rewrite the stories that stifle the energy, passion, and creativity of a family, and leverage the generative stories to establish a foundation of values and beliefs that can sustain the health of both family and business. These are generative leaders, who leave a legacy that invigorates and empowers others, laying the foundation for success across generations.

Origins of the Myth

These myths are built by the very human need to idealize our leaders. As children, the first people we idealize are our parents. To feel safe, children must believe their parents are a little more than human. After all, who will save them from the boogey man under the bed, if not *superparent*? If children saw their parents as fallible at this young age, it would create overwhelming anxiety and make it almost impossible to live. Children exist in a world that they have little control of, and they have to rely on others to navigate. The positive light of the myth of the parent calms their fears. Idealization of parents is prevalent in large part because young children tend to think in absolutes. They live in an either/or, not both/and, reality. Because they cannot integrate duality, they fail to understand that even the good guys have flaws, even Superman has his kryptonite. The stories, formed through idealization, don't allow for parental weaknesses.

As children mature, they continue to idealize parents in an effort to seek protection from those external forces that chip away security, self-worth, and purpose. This is particularly true for children whose parents are continually absent because of their leadership role in the business. Missed birthdays, failure to attend baseball games and piano recitals, absence from the everyday rituals of life—like dinner, homework and bedtime stories—can be righted by a child through idealization. A parent's absence can be filled with the story, "My dad is so important to so many people. He is serving the greater good. Of course he can't take the time to be with me!" Accepting the opposing story ("Dad is more devoted to the business than he is to me. Maybe he doesn't love me.") can lead to feelings of abandonment, self-doubt, and resentment—feelings too painful, too threatening, and too big for most to process at a young age.

The myth that children develop does not reconcile the ideal (what the world should be) to the real (what the world really is). It, in fact, distorts reality. The myth, often fed by employees as well as the community, becomes a convenient way for children to pretend not to know what they don't want to face. While a parent has had many successes, they also have flaws and vulnerabilities, and they even sometimes hurt others. Although it might be easier not to confront this reality, it is not beneficial. In fact, it is dangerous. Idealizing parents can stunt a child's ability to deal with the good and bad in others and in the world. The path to mature adulthood requires the integration of the good and bad; the development of a sense of autonomy from parents; the skills to manage emotions in the face of difficult circumstances; and the habits of forging healthy relationships with others despite their flaws. The problem with idealization—and, hence, with hero making—is that it simplifies the human experience by accounting for only the good.

Feeding the Myth

Parents often encourage the creation of these myths out of their own sense of ego, or their insecurities. Because of feelings of guilt or remorse over their failures and vulnerabilities, they encourage the creation of a mythology, and assume the role of the hero. It makes them feel like it has all been worth it. The telling of these heroic stories can bolster a sometimes-fragile ego. They can justify all of the sacrifices—like the missed birthday parties and soccer games.

In her book *Daring Greatly* (2014), Brene Brown notes that the tendencies towards narcissism are born out of the fear and vulnerability that I am not enough.[1] I am not smart enough; I'm not good looking enough. I'm not experienced enough. These insecurities can feed the parent's desire to feed the myth.

Stories also create meaning for the people surrounding the family business. The stories impart stability, as well as a sense that someone is looking out for their interests. They also communicate the values that form the culture of the organization. This culture can be a positive force guiding the behaviors of those in the system, creating a unified sense of purpose. But they can also be the source of resistance when change is needed. Rarely do family businesses grow when successors buy into the belief that the way the predecessor did things is automatically the right way.

If It Makes You Happy

Idealization also can lead to parent pleasing. "If-it-makes-dad-happy" reasoning stems from the belief that dad (who is perfect) is always right. For many family-run businesses, the "right" thing is to take over the business. It's been the (often unspoken) plan since conception. Many children have dreams and passions that exist apart from leading the business. Idealization can strap children to the business. To break free is risky. Not only might a child disappoint the parent, whose approval she's been trying to earn since childhood, but also she might invite conflict. Idealization encourages a pretend version of success. A son sees the great successes of his parents, but overlooks how his father may yell, scream, and disrespect those around him.

The successors who are able to step out of the shadows—to differentiate—aren't forced into leadership but instead have a sense of freedom. Massimo Ferragamo credits his success as a leader to his parents, who openly encouraged each child to find their calling in life. Massimo, in fact, wasn't going to join the business; "I had other things in mind," he said, like going to law school and traveling to America, where he worked at Saks 5th Avenue. After developing a sense of what he was good at and how he could better serve the company, he jumped in, operating the flagship store in the

---

[1]Brene Brown, *Daring Greatly: How the Courage to Be Vulnerable Transforms the Way We Live, Love, Parent, and Lead* (New York: Gotham Books, 2012).

United States. He says, "You have to understand your calling in life, what you should be doing, and improve upon what has been handed down to you." Children who aren't given this freedom to discover their calling might struggle to give strong, directional leadership to the family business. They might lack focus and energy because they are working out of duty rather than interest and passion.

The end result is that the myth can cause children to frame their value (who they are) in relation to their parents. No matter the effort, their successes never seem to measure up to the greatness of the parent. Their value, they believe, is doing what dad did. Take Peter, for instance, a long-standing third-generation heir in a large northwest timber business. Peter's grandfather started the business, but it was his father, Daniel, who built the business from a ten-million-dollar company to the billion-dollar company it is today. Peter's dad seemed to have the Midas touch. In reality, Peter didn't see a lot of his father growing up. Daniel tried to get to his son's football games, but often failed to show up because of a pressing business issue.

When Peter went to the office as a child, he saw how the people who worked for his dad seemed to worship him. Peter saw his dad infrequently, so he learned about the business just for an excuse to talk with his dad and visit him at the company office. His father's long track record of success, and the fact that people regaled him with great stories of his dad whenever they found out that he was Daniel Johnson's son, led Peter to believe that in order to be successful, he had to do things like dad.

His father was truly a great leader, but because of the demands of the job of the CEO, Peter was often shielded from many of the struggles and failures, fears, and doubt that had led to his dad's success. Thus, it just all seemed to magically happen.

This cost Peter a sense of who he was and what he valued. Peter's pursuit of a relationship with his dad through his pursuit of the timber business distracted Peter from what he was interested in (biology), passionate about, and good at. He said he felt a nagging sense of fear about his leadership: *How could I possibly do anything that could match what my father has done?*

The temptation to emulate one's parents is strong, almost irresistible. But my research indicates that those who succeed in taking the family business to greater heights tend to figure out at some point to lean into their strengths. They meet challenges with their vision and view of current reality rather than trying to do what dad would do. Most leaders seem to figure this out by the end of their thirties. The older one gets, the harder it is to make these shifts—the patterns become so ingrained, the belief systems hardened. During his or her twenties and thirties, the future successor's job is to wrestle with who he or she is apart from the myth he or she is born into: *How do I form my own opinion? How do I show up as an adult in my family, where I've been a kid for my entire life? Can I make the shift toward acting like an adult? Can I sit at the big boy or big girl table?*

Keeping the Next Generation in the Shadows

There are a variety of patterns that can keep a successor in the shadows, but here I will focus on three: *idealization, parentification,* and *infantalization* of the successor. Keeping a successor in the shadows is rarely a conscious decision; rather, it usually is an expression of the unconscious anxiety that a family and parents have about a family member differentiating—becoming one's own person. Subconsciously they may think, "If he doesn't emulate me, then they don't see me as worthy." So the family business system then creates a false reality through idealization, parentification, or infantalization.

Idealization of the Child

Every parent of a park district baseball team secretly believes that his son is a cut above the rest, that he just may have a shot at a professional baseball career. Every daughter has a shot at making the Olympic soccer team. It's part of the American suburban narrative. What parent doesn't believe her child is a wunderkind, a child prodigy? Parents partly (and unwittingly) countenance idealization to ensure that their children perpetuate their image. For a child to be perfect, he or she must have a perfect parent. You can see how both can become trapped in a cycle of idealization. What the child has projected on the parent ("My parent is a hero"), the parent then projects onto the child. This puts enormous external pressure on the child. It traps the child in an idealized version of what he or she really is, instead of releasing the child to experience failure and discover his or her own humanity and direction for life. As tempting as it is to idealize a child, unreflective parenting can create a story in the mind of the child that doesn't exist. One where the parent doesn't confront the child and hold him or her accountable.

That's especially true in families with successful businesses. Ultimately, founders must grapple with what they want for their children: Do you want your son to make you happy by being who you want him to be? Or do you want your daughter to be happy by being who she wants to be?

Parents who idealize their children risk raising entitled children. Think of *Tommy Boy*, the 1995 movie that chronicles the foibles of a socially and emotionally stunted successor (played by Chris Farley) following the sudden death of his industrialist father. Or any other comedic exaggeration of a successor. Depicted as entitled brats, they are emotional as well as social mutants. (Sometimes, they get their own reality shows.) The parents of such a brat spackle around the shortcoming of their parenting with the myth that they have raised a perfect child despite the flaws. However, children of parents who refuse to acknowledge their progeny's weaknesses fail to give their children what they really need—a strong sense of self. Idealization robs children of the opportunity to build self-esteem, which is constructed by coming up against barriers and overcoming them, by being held accountable, and by developing a realistic sense of who they are.

Eric Hoffer, an American moral and social philosopher, wrote in one of his notebooks on the effects of hothouse parenting, a phenomenon in which children are given endless attention by their parents. Though the parent's intent is to build self-esteem, it actually robs them of two foundational life skills: autonomy (self-governance and self-determination) and interdependence (collaboration and sharing with and real interest in others). Children, according to Hoffer, become "victims of the self-esteem trap." Parents who "make their children's needs the center of attention in every social setting" expect in return the reward of a "grown-up individual who is self-confident, empathic, loving, able to achieve whatever goals they set for themselves ... After all that parental sacrifice, according to the fictions, the children will be grateful and generous."

Hoffer concludes that sadly, "none of this works ... [because] idealization creates a home environment that cannot be reproduced in the real world. Instead of preparing our children to grow into confident and responsive adults, our unrealistic parenting leaves them mired in excessive self-concern, afraid of the challenges of adult life, and feeling bad or even defective if they don't achieve exceptional status, wealth, or accomplishments by age 28 or so."[2]

As Massimo Ferragamo says, "The toughest thing for a parent is that you have to be unpopular in order to do them good." Protecting children from their shortcomings is a shortcoming of parenting. This type of idealization can be particularly devastating for a family business.

Parentification of the Child

Idealization can lead the family to parentify the successor. Parentification is when we place a successor into a position of authority without any background or experience to be successful in this position. Now, almost all successors stepping into a new leadership role are never fully prepared to take on that role—mainly because they haven't filled that role before. But they are often chosen to lead because they have a background and track record that indicates that they can take on the new challenge. However, when a successor is parentified, the successor is set up for failure. Parentification makes a 23-year-old president of a division of the company straight out of college, merely because he or she is a family member, not because of any experience or qualifications.

Parentification puts the successor in a position of knowing at some level that he or she is not credible. It simultaneously sabotages the successor's ability to build credibility because he or she isn't prepared to do the job. In the end, this reinforces the myth because inevitably, the parent/hero must swoop back in to save the day and correct the problems. But it does not position the family business for success across generations.

Infantalization of the Successor

Infantalization is the result of a psychological need in the family to continue to view the successor as a child and not a fully-grown adult. Families can do this in many ways. They underpay the next-generation leaders, keeping successors economically dependent on their

---

[2]Polly Young-Eisendrath, "How Well Meaning Parents Cheat Their Children of Self Confidence and Self Compassion," *Psychology Today* (Sept. 16, 2011).

parents. Afraid of successors using their authority, parents keep them in lower-level positions. They don't give honest feedback. Or don't hold their children accountable for performance. All of these things keep the successor in the shadow, stunting his or her growth as a generative leader.

To prepare successors for leadership, parents must guide their children through the turbulence of growing up, exposing them to hard realities while giving them a sense of place. The trick is to root them in reality rather than suspend them in a myth.

When Massimo Ferragamo's father died, his mother took on leadership of the business. As she fully dedicated herself to the company, she never neglected her family. Massimo credits his mother for the success of all of her children: "[She] was an oak tree … letting a lot of sun and a lot of air pass through the branches, because she never did anything that was in any way impeding the growth of her sons or daughters."

If children do not have a mom (or dad) who lets the light in, they need someone to help them sort the ideal from the real. Growing into the most credible version of one's self demands bridging the gap between what is imagined and hoped for and what is true and possible. The transition from myth to reality is a transition from idealization to realization.

Idealization's Alter-Ego

The opposite of idealization is *devaluation*—the process of attributing exaggerated negative qualities to others. In many ways, devaluation is idealization's alter-ego. Both distort reality in order to make sense of a complicated reality. While idealization says the parent is all-powerful, able to solve and do anything, devaluation says the parent is a complete failure. Both help children to deal with a parent's failures (specifically, his or her mortality). In many ways, this is an attempt to differentiate. In some cases, devaluation helps children feel a sense of connection with their parent. The more human they make their parent, the more accessible they are. However, it becomes impossible to glimpse the good.

Peterson Construction was a household name in the Northeast. Bill Peterson started the company in 1960, after getting fired as a foreman from two other companies. With no college degree, but with a strong work ethic and a will to succeed, Bill built a $200 million company. The early years, however, required a great deal of sacrifice. Bill and his wife, Sharon, married shortly before they started the company in 1960 and put everything they had into the company: their money, their time, their energy, their souls. Their hard work paid off in many ways, most notably by enabling them to give the next generation whatever they needed.

While Bill Sr. was celebrated in the community for his success and contributions to the community, his son, Bill Jr., always battled with his father over the smallest issues. When he was young, it was about his allowance or curfew. When Bill Jr. entered the business, it was about budgets and how quickly Bill Jr. could advance in the company.

Bill Jr. had a long-standing resentment of his father for not being there as he was growing up. It felt to Bill like his father loved the business more than he loved his children. While the world around him saw his father as a powerful and generous man, Bill Jr. saw fault in almost everything his father did. Growing up, Bill Jr. filled his father's absence with the story that his dad was an uncaring person who was more interested in the glory of his next new building than the accomplishments or interests of his kids. Bill Jr. looked for any action that would confirm his story.

The story that Bill Jr. told himself prevented him from grasping that his father felt an enormous amount of guilt at being largely absent from his life while he was young. The resentment led Bill Jr. to rebuff his father's attempts to build a relationship with him in his teens and twenties. When Bill Jr. entered the business, their relationship worsened. Everything his father did that could be seen as harsh or uncaring was magnified. Any gesture of generosity or support was ignored.

Negative myths, like positive myths, similarly affect a successor's self-confidence and internal credibility. So engaged in the negative reaction, a child may develop a sense of victimhood. Devaluation is a fake form of differentiation. If a parent fails a child, the child expends enormous energy feeling angry at Dad rather than doing the hard work of developing internal and external credibility. Without internal credibility—a sense that he or she is meaningful and valuable—the successor can feel powerlessness over his or her problems. Creating an environment where the next generation feels entitled almost guarantees that they will feel like victims—that they have no control over their problems and deserve to be taken care of because of their last name.

Reality and True Truth

Myths and Mortals is not about failure, of course, it's about success. It's not about children climbing out of the mire of myths of their parents. It's about what makes the children of a legendary family in business build their sense of identity and establish credibility with family, employees, stakeholders, and media, and go on to become generative leaders. It is about the narrative of the successor and how they find themselves and a path to authentic leadership. Successors have to carve out their own handholds as they ascend the face of the mountain.

Every successor (and every person, for that matter) is born into a story that has been narrated collectively for many years before his or her arrival. Every person understands himself or herself in relation to these stories. The essence of right and wrong, what is valued, and how each person perceives reality is developed in relation to what is remembered and retold. The challenge is that these are stories. Though they are only perceptions of what happened, humans treat them as truth, as if they are really what happened. What exists today, however, in the here and now, are the *interpretations* of these stories. The temptation of family business successors is to tell the story of who they are in relation to the past, rather than tell new stories that portend the future. Successors who inspire others and grow stronger businesses understand that stories are merely stories. Such leaders seize the opportunity to write their own narrative while preserving the legacy of the founder.

When Salvatore Ferragamo passed away, he only produced ladies' shoes. But his dream was to create a house of luxury products, everything a man or woman would need from head to toe. Imagine if the Ferragamo children, the successors, remained stuck in the "Shoemaker of the Star" story. But the Ferragamo family wrote the second chapter of the Ferragamo story, extending the narrative Salvatore had begun. This time the story had a cast of heroes. The eldest sister introduced handbags; the second sister rolled out a ready-to-wear line; the third sister developed an accessories line, including men's ties and scarves; the second eldest brother launched a men's line. Behind the scenes, the eldest brother managed the finances and the youngest brother, Massimo, expanded the brand through advertising and marketing. All six children "pull[ed] in the same direction"—toward the dream of their father—but with skills, passion, and confidence to write their own narrative within the organization. Writing the next chapter can be summed up in Massimo's advice to successors: "Know your measure, know your size, and know where you can improve." This is truth. This is reality. This is credibility.

WHAT'S IN A NAME? (carrying the name of those who went before)

The naming of children has always fascinated me. Succession in royal families has been built on family members being named after ancestors: King Henry VII, Queen Elizabeth II. In current day, this tradition carries on in many families where one child carries the name of their mythic parent or grandparent. We see it in the case of Wrigley, where Bill's full name is William Wrigley Jr. after his grandfather. While not a guarantee of success or failure of the successor, it does tie the successor tightly to the myth.

Carrying the name John Jr. or Edward III automatically invites comparison of the successor to the mythic family figure. It makes the process of differentiation even more challenging because it inherently sends a message of following in the father's footsteps. Specifically, carrying the moniker *Junior* can imply lesser than the parent. In these cases, it is even more important for both the successor and the parent to be vigilant in helping successors find space and distance to establish their own sense of identity and their own authentic leadership style.

CASE EXAMPLE: Karl-Erivan Haub, CEO of Tengelmann Group

"My son carries the same name as my father. We keep passing on the name, Karl-Erivan, Erivan Karl, so we keep switching that four or five generations now. So, now [people in the community] would know us because the name is not very common in Germany. And since you frequently read it in the paper, the next generation can have difficulties. . . . My son was once embarrassed by his teacher, by calling him out and talking about "your father: and the supermarket around the corner needs to be run better. Maybe your father invites me to run it."

Through no fault of his own, a young man in school, just trying to learn, is pulled into the story of the family business. Whether we like it or not, the shadow often follows us. It is for us to prepare successors to deal with these challenges.

CHAPTER

2

Out of the Shadows

The journey of the successor to lead apart from the myth

"**W**ith your stupid ideas, six months after I die you're going to blow up this business."

That is how Nick Perrino, who built Home Run Inn from a small tavern to a 600-seat restaurant, motivated his son, Joe, as he attempted to step out of the shadow of his father's success.

Nick feared the changes his son pushed for: from smaller changes like implementing a shirt and tie dress code for employees, or introducing booth space to create more seating; to the weightier ones, such as partnering with other companies to grow the company, or automating a manufacturing plant to mass produce its iconic frozen pizza.

"My own father didn't think I would succeed," says Joe Perrino, CEO of Home Run Inn.

Founded by Nick's in-laws, Italian immigrants Mary and Vincent Grittani, Home Run Inn began as a small southside Chicago tavern that dished up a little piece of Italy—fresh, hot, and free pizza—to its bar patrons. The tavern, whose name, as legend has it, was born after a game-winning home run shattered the tavern's front window, was symbolic of the convergence of the Old World and New. While running the tavern was a swing at the American dream, the family guarded its Italian heritage. Three generations of the Grittani-Perrino family lived behind the restaurant.

"We would have lunch in the kitchen of the restaurant," says Joe, "and Easter dinner in the restaurant dining room." During the early years, Home Run Inn was less about building wealth than about preserving a heritage and providing a future for a family, whose impoverished family in the Old World was considered the lowest class—peasant farmers.

When Nick Perrino took over the business after the death of his father-in-law, he never envisioned growing it into the top-selling frozen pizza company in Chicago that it is today.

That took the "stupid" ideas of his son, Joe.

Like the baseball that shattered the tavern's window, Joe shattered the old way of doing business. Nick had kept the business alive during the Al Capone and Bugs Moran era. He sought to do business honestly in a world of gangsters, bribes, and extortion, where business was all about protecting what one had. It was a principle carried from his impoverished days in Italy.

Joe recounts a time he wanted to change their bread supplier. "My dad said, 'If you do that, they come after our restaurant.' Dad believed that we needed to act poor, that pizza was for peons, and his oft-repeated advice to live by was to 'associate with someone better than you, and pay the expense.'"

This was the "gospel of Perrino," says Joe. "He was a leader in the community, a politician. He held a meeting every Monday, and politicians came from all over. He could have been a congressman."

When Joe came into leadership, he kicked the kowtowing. Authorities would write up the restaurant for a violation, looking for a take. Instead of paying them off, Joe fixed the problem. The notion that success is built on the association with others better than you was, according to Joe, no better "than a myth."

"They're not all they're cracked up to be, you know?" Joe says.

This self-confidence was earned early on. Joe was one of the top athletes in the area. America's favorite pastime was Joe's favorite pastime, and while playing baseball he developed the confidence to lead. On the diamond, he took a manager's approach to the game. "I became captain, and would hire and fire kids from the team." His confidence was matched by decisiveness, which prompted Joe, at the age of 18, to make a career decision that would save his father from making a fateful one.

"He was going to sell the business to our bookkeeper for $200,000. And I said, 'Dad, I'll come in, and I'll [run] it.'"

Joe switched his major from dentistry to business and graduated from Lewis University, where he recruited three other graduates to help him expand Home Run Inn into a business enterprise with locations throughout the city.

"I was gung-ho to open up more places," says Joe. "And then ... nothing happened. We just stayed in the same place and got bigger."

From 1975 to 1987, the restaurant grew exponentially, from 40 seats to 300 to 600. But for Joe it wasn't enough. From his perspective, it was 12 years of doing the same thing over and over. Joe says that the frozen pizza business was something his father never wanted to be in. But Joe forged ahead. By the time Joe hit his early forties, the frozen pizza business hit a home run. And Joe had secured his spot as rightful leader.

In order to take Home Run Inn to the next level, Joe had to find his own way to lead. He had to step out of the mythology of his father, respecting Nick's values while reinventing the business for the future. It is what all successors must do to lead the business into a new era. "Some things [my father] did very, very well," says Joe. Nick invested in relationships and in the community. "Other things," says Joe, "we had to break through as a family culture." One of them was the dominating fear that curtailed the business from expanding. Nick Perrino led in a way consistent with his identity—for the good and the bad: his inherent personality traits, life experiences (like living through the Depression), second-grade education, family values, Italian heritage, and generational influences all combined to shape his values, and consequently, approach to life and leadership. The perspectives of father and son were as distant from one another as the Old World was from the New.

Nick had always looked at the pizza business and saw its limitations; his son looked at it and saw opportunity for innovation, growth, and success. Nick wanted the best for his son, and for him that meant encouraging him to pursue something different than what he considered the lowbrow pizza industry. Joe respected his father, and for him that meant doing the same thing his dad did, but differently. "My father had the leadership style of a dictator—my way only, volatile and explosive when it didn't go his way," says Joe, "I was an ambassador seeking peace and harmony to achieve our goals."

Joe Perrino had a more nuanced and constructive understanding than his father did of what it meant to be different. He was able to integrate the best of what his father had done with what he knew would make it exponentially better. This stemmed in part from his personality, brimming with self-confidence and the ability to take command of a situation.

The conflict that Joe experienced with his father is a natural part of the succession process. In order for successors to step out of the shadows of their parents, they have do try to do things differently, in a way that is authentic to them. To do things differently is to invite conflict. No parent or successor should be disheartened by the presence of conflict in the succession process. Conflict is inherent in succession. To truly step into leadership, the successor must chafe against his predecessor's way of doing things. What should be assessed is how healthy that conflict is.

These conflicts are the seeds of a term first coined by psychologist Murray Bowen called *differentiation*. As I discussed in the previous chapter, this is the normal process of an individual developing their sense of self in relation to others. One of the primary relationships in the differentiation process is separating one's identity from the parent. Assessing one's level of differentiation involves evaluating one's own ability to think and act for oneself in the presence of highly charged emotion. And there is no relationship more emotionally charged than that of parent and child.

As Joe sought to differentiate from his father by trying to do things differently, his father resisted, calling him stupid. In a way, Nick was saying "How dare you not be me." The reality is that for any successor to step out of the shadows and become a truly authentic and generative leader, he must dare to *not* be like the predecessor.

Despite his father's swirling negativity, Joe excelled in the pursuit of differentiation. He developed a strong sense of self. In fact, as he created his own definition of success, the family business experienced explosive growth.

Developing a sense of self, such as Joe did, is to understand one's uniqueness. From that comes the self-confidence to believe that our contribution is necessary precisely because it is different. We can contribute something that no one else can. This is critical for the successor in a family business who must differentiate in the presence of the predecessor. Do the same thing (lead the family business), but differently (as only he or she can).

Differentiation and the Life Cycle

The first challenge of differentiation is attending to the challenges of human development at each of life's cycles as children grow up; this is how the "self" emerges. Life cycle theory[1] suggests there are primary tasks a human must accomplish during different stages of his or her development in order to become a fully mature adult. It is believed that failure to accomplish a primary task at any one of these stages will result in behavioral struggles later in life.[2] A successor who fails to differentiate has likely struggled to accomplish one or more of these tasks. In many cases, a successor's ability to successfully move through each life cycle, from dependence to independence, is shaped largely by his or her parental influence. Here is a brief overview.[3]

Attending (0 to 18 months)

At this phase, a child's primary task is to develop a sense that he or she is loved and, hence, valuable. When crying is shushed with a feeding, a changed diaper, or a gentle rocking, a child's worth is affirmed. Random (rather than consistent) interaction results in either the child exhibiting little or no expression (he or she has learned that her needs will go unnoticed) or the child crying consistently (he or she will clamor for his or her needs to be met).

Power (18 to 36 Months)

This is the stage at which children learn that they have influence over the world. A child, for instance, will break his sister's toy and delight in it; he sees the power he has over the world around him. Because he has not developed a conscience, however, he shows no remorse. In seeing the relationship of their actions to others, children at this stage begin to distinguish themselves from others.

Responsibility and Conscience (36 months to 5 years)

Developing responsibility is the primary task at this stage. The same child will take his sister's toy and begin to show remorse, recognizing his behavior impacts others. Guilt and remorse are the seeds of a growing conscience.

---

[1] Erik Erikson, *Identity and the Life Cycle* (Madison, CT: International University Press, 1959).

[2] D. Levinson, *Seasons of a Man's Life* (New York: Random House, 1978).

[3] E. Monte, Lecture, Loyola University Chicago Family Business Center. 2014.

Competency and Latency (5 or 6 to 11 years)

During this stage of the life cycle, children begin to see themselves as competent human beings. They learn they are good at some things that others struggle to master. Problems often surface later in life when parents tell a child he or she is good at something that the child isn't actually good at it.

This is also the stage when children identify gender. A pre-adolescent boy, for instance, will realize he is different from his mother and turn toward his father. It is critical at this stage that the father helps his son understand what it is to be different from mom. And if the father is absent—because he is focusing on the business—it might create a struggle for young boys.

Separation and Adolescence (12 to 23 years)

Separation from parents and family begins at this stage. This is when an adult identity and real sense of self begins to form. Rebellion in this stage is often about being "not" mom or "not" dad. It is about preparing for adulthood.

Early Adulthood (20s and 30s)

This is the stage at which we begin to explore the world and our place in it. It's about finding the balance between connecting to others, finding meaningful work, and having a sense of separation without being isolated.[4] Because a sense of responsibility and commitment is developed, it is at this stage that individuals most typically establish their own families. Tasks not accomplished in earlier stages may negatively show up in one's efforts to marry and create a family. Leaning too much toward intimacy, an individual risks losing herself in another person. The healthy approach is to develop a sense of reciprocal love with another.

Through many years of working with successors in our Next Generation Leadership Institute and other programs at Loyola University Chicago, I have learned that successors and parents who do not adequately attend to the challenges presented at each of the life stages most often get stuck in the shadow and resist the natural process of differentiation. If a successor, for instance, fails to develop a sense of

---

[4]D. Levinson, *Seasons of a Man's Life* (New York: Random House, 1978).

responsibility, a sense of competency, or a healthy sense of separation from his or her parents, stepping out of the shadows is difficult if not impossible.

Anytime successors are stuck in their role or development, reflecting on whether any of the core tasks of development were missed, and what was happening in their lives at the time, can shed meaning and help the successors get unstuck.

Overcoming the Successor's Curse

All successors carry a burden. They most always are appraised in relationship to their predecessors and their family. This is called the *successor's curse*. Failures are often magnified in comparison to the predecessors, and their successes aren't seen as their own. Differentiation is the curse's cure.

To lead the company that his father built from one restaurant to a chain of restaurants to a manufacturing juggernaut, Joe Perrino had to map out his own path to leadership. He had to assert himself—take risks. This requires the pursuit of differentiation, discovering one's true self, and is the foundational work of becoming a generative successor.

Differentiation follows a unique path for each successor, based on a composite of personality, family patterns, biology, generational influences, education, and societal context. Joe's never-back-down personality and tenacity for trying new things chaffed against his father's more conservative personality. These qualities in part were innate and in part shaped by the socioeconomics and time period to which each were born. Unlike his father, Joe grew up on the proverbial field of dreams. America afforded limitless possibilities. And while he heard the stories of his ancestors scraping by through the Depression, he only knew the prosperity on the other side. Business ventures that seemed risky and irresponsible to Nick were necessary and fundamental investments in the future according to Joe. For Joe to lead the way his father had would have been inauthentic, and, possibly, detrimental to the family business. Both Nick and Joe had their own context and time.

As Massimo Ferragamo, successor to Ferragamo USA, pointed out: The danger of thinking that you can be just like your parents is a failure to "understand what your calling is in life, what you should be doing, and how to improve on what has been given to you." Each successor must undergo a crisis of identity. In this crisis, the emerging leader faces the risk of losing herself in their predecessor's myth. The leader will be forced to confront the impression that he or she is a carbon copy of the predecessor. At this pivotal moment, a successor can choose to step away from the myth and towards his or her authentic self. It is first an internal shift (that demands self-reflection) and then an external shift (that requires experimentation) away from the self that is scripted by the myth.

Successors who shortcut this process are commonly ineffective leaders. They capitulate to external influences as well as the expectations others have of them. They are emotionally immature and manifest behavior more typical of tyrants:

- They are volatile and highly emotional in conflict.
- They crave the approval of others.
- When criticized, they become highly emotional, subject to big mood swings.
- They allow others to excessively influence their decisions.
- They preserve their own ego at the expense of others.
- They have difficulty hearing and empathizing with other opinions and ideas.
- They take credit to feed their own egos.
- They develop a sense of entitlement.

Differentiation can be manifested in small but important ways. When Joe first stepped into a leadership role at the restaurant, he found himself in the kitchen, wearing an apron and hat, tossing pizzas. During the early years, Joe dreamed of expanding the business to include mass production of frozen pizzas. But no one took Joe's ideas seriously. He suffered the successor's curse: "I was the son of the owner … always living in the shadows. People would say, 'You'd be nothing without your dad. You're riding on your dad's coattails.'" In order to step out of the shadow, Joe realized he had to earn credibility. It began with a small, seemingly insignificant, choice of attire.

One day Joe showed up to work in a shirt and tie. All the old-time managers, as Joe puts it, thought it was a joke. Day after day, Joe donned the shirt and tie, regardless of the sneering. Joe's thought was, "I have to change my image if I'm going to change the whole business." After about five years, everyone started wearing a uniform—even his dad's old guys started wearing a shirt and tie.

This one small step outside his father's shadow changed Joe's image as well as the image of the business. By the time his father passed away, all the old timers had fallen in line with Joe's leadership. And a few years later, the frozen pizza business was starting to scale.

To escape the founder's or predecessor's shadow, a young leader must understand the current reality of the existing business; determine what needs to change; and figure out if he or she is fit for the job. In my experience, those who make a successful transition tend to be reflective. They ask:

- What are my personal values?
- What am I good at?
- What am I passionate about?
- What do I want for my life and my career?
- What does the family enterprise need from me? Am I prepared to provide that?
- Do my personal values align with the family business?

There must be alignment between who a successor is and what the business needs. A successor may be good at something, but if he or she is not passionate about it, or if the family business doesn't need it, then succession is difficult for both successor and the family business.

To lead with credibility, successors take the risk to lead as only they can lead. They must develop core convictions and form their own values and vision for their life, all while honestly assessing if they possess what the business needs going forward.

A turning point is when a young leader grasps fully that what allowed the organization to succeed in the past might not help the organization meet the challenges of the future. This is confidence earned through the differentiation process. By doing things the way a parent did or approves of, a successor fails to develop her own sense of what is right.

From Hero to Human: Deconstructing the Myth of the Founder

For successors to become generative leaders, they must downsize their ego—from hero to human. It is hard to do this without meeting the challenges of life cycle development. As they humanize themselves—taking ownership of both the good and bad parts of themselves—they are then equipped to humanize their predecessor.

They can integrate their good with the bad and develop empathy for their predecessors' failures and vulnerabilities as well as their own. This doesn't mean they ignore their predecessors' successes, but they contextualize those successes.

Although parents don't set out to be their child's hero, they can fall into the trap of accepting the role of hero. What parent doesn't want to be known as a person of conviction, perseverance, courage, sacrifice, and compassion? It is instinctive to want to be recognized by the family as the one who made it happen, who made the sacrifice. The problem comes when a parent allows a child to idealize these qualities, sheltering him or her from failure, conflict, and the hard-knocks of life. Allowing hero-making may inhibit the more mundane but critical responsibilities of parenting, such as instilling values into the child. By focusing on values as opposed to passively and tacitly reinforcing the myth, the parent communicates stability to the child. Doing so also provides continuity with the family values that drive the business.

The stories parents use to instruct are particularly compelling because while they are lessons in legend, they are also lessons in life. A story is compelling and instructive when it conveys a value. Bob Vermeer, chairman emeritus, and his sister Mary Andringa, CEO and Chair of the Vermeer Corporation, recall their father openly talking about his failures, like the gravedigger machine that didn't work, or the time they developed a mowing machine before John Deere, but weren't able to get it to market because of distribution rights. A measure of a parent's self-confidence is his or her ability to be honest about the failures and not react to failures with harshness and blame. And every successful family business has many of them. In the process of becoming a differentiated adult, successors must see their parents as more than just the hero. They need to see the parent as human.

A myth of a legendary figure without the raw stories of that person's humanity, flaws, and weaknesses only enlarges the legend while shortening the legacy. If the essence of idealizing is the making of a hero, the task of stepping out of the shadow is the unmaking of a hero. This does not mean diminishing the hero and what he or she has accomplished. Nor does it mean demonizing the hero—making the hero a villain. Rebellion is a fake version of differentiation. It makes the parent all bad, rather than integrating both good and bad. Deconstructing the myth of a hero humanizes the person. It strips back the veneer, revealing his or her mistakes while accepting, learning from, and even forgiving the failures. Coming to grips with the mortality of a parent gives successors a realistic sense of who they are, freeing up emotional energy to be more forgiving of themselves. It also gives them a shot at taking their own path, and the freedom to not emulate the parent.

Heroes can't be followed if there is no humanity to learn from and build on. The task of the successor in a family business is to acknowledge the legend while continuing to build the legacy in a way that the legendary figure might have never envisioned—but in a way that bears the imprint of the successor.

But to do this, the successor must "leave home," the very place where the shadow is greatest. In leaving, a child gains the necessary distance from the idealized hero. After a stint in the "real world," such as Massimo Ferragamo's travels to America, a child can return to see his or her parent-hero in a different light. Rather than following an appointed path, a script for life with predictable steps, a child who goes off-script creates experiences that will help to define an identity apart from the myth. This is the task of recognizing who you aspire to be in light of who your parents are or were: their successes, what they did for you, what they passed on to you, and what they challenged you to reach for. But it also means realizing who you are in light of your own gifts, skills, and passion. A child who finds his or her own sense of calling is better able to resist the pull into the predecessor's shadow.

I liken it to body building. The best way to tone your body is by pushing against something, allowing resistance to develop strength and definition. So, too, the best way to develop a productive and healthy relationship is to allow for resistance between generations. Resistance is the middle ground between compliance and rebellion. It is the common ground between parent and child, predecessor and successor, on which the business can continue to grow. Part of growing up, and growing into a strong leader, is learning to outgrow the hero complex, moving beyond the mythic ideal of the parent–savior. Both parents (the heroes) and successors (the ones rescued) must learn this.

Succession can be messy because differentiation inevitably causes conflict. As the successor leans into a way of leading that is authentic to him or her, he or she pushes against the predecessor's proven way of leading. Differentiated leaders understand that conflict kicks up emotion that needs to be reconciled with the facts.

They are empathetic to others' perspectives and points of view, but they avoid sympathy. Empathy seeks understanding; sympathy wants solidarity. Differentiated leaders don't get sucked in even when they receive negative feedback. They pursue what they feel is in the best interest of the whole, and don't allow negative emotion to sway them. Strong successors are able to step out from the shadows cast by parents and grandparents that are often laden with emotion, entitlement, and expectation: the Silver Spoon Club. Released from the burden, they are free to develop their own identity. They become the hub of family legacy that champions the best of the family values and leverages the strengths of its members. Together, the family generates meaning, purpose, and an emotional return of investment—all the things that money can't buy.

The Bowen Center for the Study of the Family describes this differentiated leader as one who:

> Recognizes his realistic dependence on others, but he can stay calm and clear headed enough in the face of conflict, criticism, and rejection to distinguish thinking rooted in a careful assessment of the facts from thinking clouded by emotionality. Thoughtfully acquired principles help guide decision-making about important family and social issues, making him less at the mercy of the feelings of the moment. What he decides and what he says matches what he does. He can act selflessly, but his acting in the best interests of the group is a thoughtful choice, not a response to relationship pressures. Confident in his thinking, he can either support another view without being a disciple or reject another view without polarizing the differences. He defines himself without being pushy and deals with pressure to yield without being wishy-washy.

This can feel threatening, even disorienting, to a successor. He can act selflessly, but it must be a thoughtful choice, not a response to relationship pressures. Breaking away from the old patterns is a sign that the successor has done the hard work of figuring out what he or she believes—determining what to hold onto to preserve the identity of the business, and what fresh perspective is necessary to lead the business into the next era.

When Successors Chart Their Own Course

Creating one's own definition of success as distinct from that of one's parents, family, and business community is a primary task of differentiation. What distinguishes successful successors in family businesses is their ability to chart their own course. On a journey to identity formation, signposts mark the way, indicating, "Stop! You're headed in the wrong direction!" or, "Keep going in this direction." Trials faced through experimentation; overcoming failures; feedback from others; mentors; education: These all provide the successors with feedback that they are headed in the right (or wrong) direction.

The strength to define a unique course of action comes from a clear understanding that we are more than who our parents want us to be. And sometimes, from their point of view, less than they want us to be. While many young leaders focus their actions on making their parents happy, the most successful successors do things differently, despite disapproval from their parents. Identity is formed through differentiation, enabling a successor to achieve internal as well as external credibility. The more he or she aligns her beliefs with her actions, the more credibility he or she experiences. To quote Dave Juday, retired chairman of Ideal Industries, this can help the successor "start with what needs to be done, rather than what has always been done."

The family mythology often works against this, trapping individuals into roles along with familial versions of success. It's hard to break free from the roles, because underlying the roles is a child's primal wish for parental acceptance and love. The child will tend to give primary consideration to the way parents see him or her, not the way the child sees him- or herself. The task of self-awareness is asking, "How do I see myself?" and, "What does success look like for me?" One can only imagine where Home Run Inn would be today had Joe Perrino bought into his father's assessment that all Joe's ideas were stupid.

Defining self apart from one's parents doesn't happen overnight, but gradually as one differentiates. Determining what's right for the future is largely dependent on the cultivation of self-confidence, wisdom, and knowledge, which I will discuss in chapters to come. These are all necessary to make this break from the parent. Cultivating a gut instinct, identifying his or her passion, knowing his or her strengths and weaknesses, and working toward continual improvement—all lay the foundation for a successor to choose to do things in a way that is authentic to him- or herself.

Unintentionally, successors fail to lead authentically because they fail to differentiate. It is all too easy to assume the larger identity of legendary parents and to allow that to prop up the leader's sense of self. But it's only a crutch. Successors can't build a foundation of credibility on someone else's accomplishments. The foundation of authenticity can only be built from the hard work of establishing a true sense of one's self and one's own accomplishments.

When Idealization Interferes

The first draft of the story of a person's life is written by the genes during fetal development. That's nature. Parents help to shape the rough draft, filling in the narrative during childhood. That's nurture. But nature and nurture can only take the story so far. Sooner or later, the individual has to take authorship to develop fully the story's main character—him- or herself.

For all the ways a myth provides meaning and purpose, it rarely helps the successor establish a strong sense of self. The myth a successor grows up with is likely to confuse the issue of identity. One dead end that I have identified (see Chapter 1) is *idealization*, the process of exaggerating positive qualities in a person. Children naturally idealize their parents, and parents tend to also idealize their children, especially when they confuse loving their children with loving the best of themselves in their children. What parents often want is their own image reflected by their children, not someone who is uniquely different from them. The irony is that it is the child's uniqueness and sense of self that will allow him or her to lead the business with credibility, and consequently further the family legacy.

The natural progression of succession in a family business is that parents foist their expectations on their children. The expectations become the obligations of the child, who works from a sense of duty rather than desire. One successor once said to me regarding his choice to enter the business: "I felt that if I didn't come into the business, I would be letting my father down."

The process of idealization can also go the way of indulgence, of setting no expectations at all, except for that of happiness, and providing for their children a canvass of unlimited potential and opportunity: "You can do anything. I just want you to be happy."

Both specific expectation and suspended expectation present dilemmas to a successor trying to figure out who he is and what he wants. The one defines the successor by his duty: "I will be the loyal child, the good soldier, and do what's expected." The other leaves all identity open: "You can do and be anything." Neither guides children into a growing sense of their own personhood.

The statements, "I am doing what my parents want me to do," or, "I can do anything I want to do," leave the successor asking the same question: "What is it that I *want* to do?" While the temptation might be to see differentiation as solely the challenge of the successor, the parent also plays a powerful role in the process. If the parents work to give the next-generation leaders a true understanding of their strengths and weaknesses, as well as their successes and their failures, this can let light through the shade of the tree.

Shining the Light Inward

The inner work of self-awareness can be prompted by intuition, but it must become an intentional process of getting to know what is underneath the surface. It demands figuring out one's own personhood. A successor must compare the story of who he thinks he is with the reality of who he is—and be honest about the gap. Building internal credibility starts with this self-awareness, the inner work that only the leader can see that validates the outer work that everybody else sees.

It's not just turning on the light, but intentionally shining it inward and asking, "What am I not seeing?" as well as, "What am I pretending not to know?" Successors must find the courage to face the most realistic version of who they are. Self-awareness is something that builds and grows across the life cycle. Unfortunately, it can be distorted by the messages of our parents and the shadow. A temptation for Joe Perrino might have been to believe his father's opinion that his ideas were stupid, but he worked hard to differentiate in spite of this. Self-awareness is also a learned characteristic. It develops over time. The process of development ranges from obliviousness (having little or no understanding of one's own emotions), to consciousness (individuals become aware not only of who they are, but who they are in the mind of others). Self-awareness is innate; it is learned; and it must also be applied.

Differentiating oneself from one's parents starts with self-awareness. Self-awareness is the process of building consciousness of "who I really am in the world." Rather than just implementing a parent's or the family's vision for the successor's future, as a successor becomes self-aware she becomes clear about who she wants to be, what she is passionate about, and what she is good at—who she *really* is. It's about creating a clear vision of who one wants to be in the world, and reconciling that with who one really is. To be self-aware is to increase one's understanding of what one values, personality, style, the impressions that one leaves on others, what one is good at and, where one needs to improve. Through building self-awareness, a successor can begin to own his own definition of success—one that builds on the best of the family legacy, while charting a course that is true to his or her unique talents and beliefs. This work can be both practical and reflective.

The following describes four practical ways a successor can increase self-awareness:

1. **Personality inventories.** These provide feedback about personality traits and styles and offer information that can help the individual understand the implications for their personality in leadership and family interactions. Some of the most common include DISC, Myers Briggs, The Hogan, Big Five, and Strength Finders.

2. **360 reviews.** 360-degree review processes are designed to give leaders feedback from those with whom they interact. Through a structured survey and/or interview process, a 360 gathers real feedback about others' perceptions of one's strengths, weaknesses, and leadership style. Commonly, bosses, peers, and direct reports provide feedback. The 360 can be either transparent or anonymous, but the data collected from others is then compared to the successors' own ratings of themselves.

3. **Coaching.** Trained coaches work with leaders to help clarify professional as well as personal goals. Using personality inventories and 360 reviews, coaches develop a practical game plan to achieve those goals and maneuver around roadblocks.

4. **Taking action.** By taking action and interacting in the world, we get feedback about who we are and what we are good at. The more we act and interact, the more we learn.

Reflection is much more introspective, psychological, and nonlinear. These methods require successors to reflect on the knowledge that they have about themselves, as well as the feedback they get from others, and then determine what needs to change in their life because of the information. These reflective methods are often needed to fully integrate the feedback provided by the more practical methods of building self-awareness. Reflective methods include these three:

1. **Journaling.** The simple process of writing down thoughts and periodically reviewing them offers an initial degree of self-reflection that can provide perspective.
2. **Meditation/mindfulness.** These methods focus on building one's self-awareness by focusing on the here and now, paying attention to what is happening in the moment.
3. **Therapy.** Although often stigmatized, therapy can be an invaluable tool for leaders to understand how the patterns and traumas in their lives impact their relationships and leadership in the here and now.

Building one's sense of identity through self-awareness allows the successor to build both internal and external credibility, which I will explore in subsequent chapters. Along with the discovery of one-self as a unique entity comes the understanding of independence to exert one's will and either adopt, adapt, or discard that which surrounds the leader. For the emerging leader, this is about testing his or her capabilities against reality. For lack of hard data about oneself, an individual will make up a version of self that doesn't necessarily match reality. The more self-aware a successor becomes, the better able the individual is to make an informed assessment of what he or she is capable of.

Bella Hoare is a banker—a career she admits rarely makes any child's "What I Want to Be When I Grow Up" list. Bella is an eleventh-generation managing partner of the family-owned C. Hoare & Co.: "Private bankers since 1672."[5] C. Hoare & Co. is the oldest bank in the United Kingdom, the world's fifth oldest bank, and the most profitable in the country.

According to Bella, she wasn't born to be a banker; she certainly wasn't interested in a banking career. Instead, she grew into it as she

---

[5]Hutchings, Victoria (2005). *Messrs Hoare Bankers: A History of the Hoare Banking Dynasty.* Constable and Robinson, Ltd. London.

worked to become the person she wanted to be. Now, banking is an expression of her personality. "I don't make the distinction between business and my personal values, some of which are different, particularly in the banking world. ... I'm a firm believer in having fun. It's one of my core values. There's not a lot of fun in banking."

Bella developed a sense of fun, in part, from the way her parents raised her. "They never boxed me in," she says. "If you box people in ... then things explode."

On the one hand, Bella says she was not "really taught anything growing up," but when she talks about her parents, she reveals their profound influence on her. "I was difficult, awkward, and generally grungy and revolting," she says, "but my parents never excluded me. My father never made me do anything, but when he said, 'I suggest,' I knew it came with the full weight of his parental authority." He also brought to bear the weight of a father's love. When Bella went away to boarding school, he wrote her every week, "and every letter he told me stories about people in his life, but never about work." He shared himself as a human more than a hero.

Her father's presence, strong but not dominating, gave Bella freedom to explore what she valued. She was burdened by neither expectations nor idealization. "I didn't grow up," she says, "being told I was clever or beautiful or anything like that on any sort of regular basis. But I always knew my own mind." And her own values. As her teacher reported, "We hope that next term Arabella will see homework as more than an intrusion into her valued private life."

Bella idled through school and then hit the throttle into her career. She followed her half-Russian husband to his half-motherland, learned Russian so she could work for a stock brokerage firm where she was hired as number 2 of 2, and stayed until she was number 2 of 75. All the while, Bella was preparing herself for the job that she didn't want.

Her cousin, Alex Hoare, was managing partner of the bank, and Bella had been a luminary on his radar. For one year he pursued her, and she rebuffed him. "Why should I come to a dozy family firm on Fleet Street?" she says. As it turned out, Alex got his way, and so did Bella.

Bella ascribes to the theory that mistakes are strategic, not chronic. You don't keep making the same ones. "I learned a lot of lessons from the mistakes I made at my two jobs, and none here knows about those mistakes. They can see that I've learned." Bella has proved herself to the one man who matters the most: her father. "He has seen me make useful comments, understanding the issues, taking the business forward. It's been a process of adjustment, from viewing me as Little Bella, to the person he trusts to hold his company in her hands."

"Taking it forward" is Bella's life approach. "Your job expands at the rate of your capabilities." For Bella, that includes opportunities that she has seized and created for herself. These have included taking a course at Harvard, seeing a therapist ("very un-English" she laughs), finding mentors at work, and drawing strength from a community of friends. "You end up reasonably confident," she says, "that you understand your strengths and weaknesses." She had a strong sense of self, and continued to build it so that at the peak of her career, her "self" and her work coalesced. "I don't make a distinction between a business life and a personal set of values," she says. "And some of those values are different."

Different indeed. Bella Hoare has made banking fun, and that perhaps, is her greatest achievement.

Asserting the Self in the Family Legacy

For the young leaders in a family business, self-awareness is a journey that must happen within the context of the family legacy. They are more than sons and daughters; they are stewards of the larger social organism, which the family has produced. The emphasis is not merely on individual success ("What am I going to do with my life?") but also on the family mission ("What role do I want to play in helping the family achieve its goals?"). It was in this context that Bill Wrigley made his declaration of independence, "I am not my father," and coupled it with a declaration of differentiation from his father, "I am going to do things differently." Differentiation is what allows the successor to "honor the past while doing what's best for the future."

But there is no formula. While Bella worked outside the family business and returned later, others have worked in the business and earned their way to the top, like Joe Perrino. For John Tyson of Tyson Foods, Inc., the process of differentiation is founded on a simple philosophy: "You just work." John never consciously joined the family business, because he was never away from it. "The only succession here at Tyson Foods," says John, "would be those who worked hard and got a chance to do more." John got his chance at 13, working at just about every job that Tyson had, under the tutelage of many of its employees. One experience in particular shaped his understanding of the company, his place in it, and the way he would run it when he became CEO. At 16, he was assigned one of the simpler jobs at the plant, taking chicken crates full of chickens off the upper conveyor belt on the truck and putting them on a lower conveyor belt. The manager showed him how to do it, but John wasn't paying attention. On his first chicken-crate transfer, wet chicken litter sprayed his face.

"What do I do now?" John asked.

"You just stay here and work. I'm going back to the office."

The manager came back at lunch with a new pair of jeans and a T-shirt that he had purchased at the local dry goods store. "He knew I wasn't paying attention," says John, "and that I was going to get broadsided with chicken s—t. And he knew that he was going have to buy me a change of clothes. He was paying attention to the details, and he took care of me because I was his employee."

Caring for his employees became one of John Tyson's core values, which he learned not just from his father but from the workers at Tyson. The greatest differentiator for John was both the variety of jobs that he did and the diversity of people for whom he did them: "They all contribute to the mosaic of who I am today."

Successors find out who they are as they interact with others, become aware of their strengths, work, gain feedback, pick themselves up after failure, experiment with leadership, and push against the established way of doing things, which I will discuss in the chapters to come. Every successor does it differently, and at different times in their lives. Bella kicked against the system from the moment she was born, furiously defying who she wasn't. She began the positive work of differentiation when she resisted the pull of the family business and found her own career path, along with "the really good fun of succeeding because you've worked hard." For some leaders, like Bill Wrigley Jr., stepping out of the shadow comes years after unsuccessfully emulating the successor. Other leaders, like Joe Perrino, challenge the successor's business practices prior to taking on the mantle of leadership.

Being born into a myth that provides meaning and purpose is the beneficence of nature. And it is followed by all the nurture of blessings that an iconic family enterprise bestows on the successor. But a successor will only find self-fulfillment in the organization when he figures out what he can uniquely contribute to the ongoing legacy. Differentiation starts this process, and value formation continues it.

Perhaps that is one of the most important markers that signals an emerging leader will be successful—he or she changes a value or emphasizes a value over another. She doesn't merely parrot the values of the predecessor. The leader brings unique convictions to bear on the family business. Values are the core principles, the inner convictions that leaders aspire to live by and that guide behavior. A leader's actions are either in alignment with her values or they aren't. A leader who has stepped out of the shadows will risk the consequences of becoming aligned with his values, even when that means change for the family business.

Joe Perrino stepped out of the shadows by challenging his father's conservative approach to business, even if it led to disapproval. "I challenged [my father] on anything that he'd say. I would ask him, 'Why do we have to do it that way?' And he would get real upset." Just as Nick wished Joe would quiet his crazy ideas, so Joe wished his father would have been "open-minded and progressive—because they could have been so much more." To lead in lockstep with his father would have been inauthentic to Joe. By nature, Joe was a competitor, not a survivor. "You have to want to compete," he says, "and you have to want to be the best." So Joe did things his dad would never do, like automating the first frozen pizza plant, joining a presidents' forum to network, and meeting with competitors to open the door to future opportunities.

Aligning his actions with his values—that's how Joe went from "a stupid kid that rode on his daddy's coattails" to the Home Run king.

CHAPTER

3

You Gotta Earn It

Earning your way to the top

In 1974, Christie Hefner was the quintessential feminist, a Brandeis graduate with an interest in law, politics, and journalism. And a decided disinterest in business.

"Liberals in my generation," she says, "felt that business was, at the very least, suspect, if not the enemy. . . . They didn't care about human rights."

It seems that Christie's father, Hugh Hefner, founder of Playboy Enterprises, would have been public enemy number one: a man who made his fortune selling sexy women. But he wasn't. Playboy in fact supported many women's rights causes. In 1975, after a year of working for the Boston Phoenix, Christie took a job at Playboy, and a few years later, an opportunity arose. In 1982, Playboy was in trouble. While the board was thinking of searching for an outsider, Christie made a proposal to Hef and the board that she step in (rather than delay with the search for an outsider) and form an office of the President. She felt she had a sense that she knew what needed to be done and that she already had the trust of being a family member. Before too long she was making command decisions at the company. A liberal feminist was calling the shots for the ultimate boy's club. It was an eyebrow-raising succession, as Christie pointed out, that generated "a certain amount of press." Though as a feminist she entered the business with what she calls a "certain level of disability," Christie managed to shatter the glass ceiling before the masses knew what a glass ceiling was. Then in 1988, after Hef had a stroke and felt that he no longer wanted to have the role of CEO, she succeeded her father as CEO of Playboy.

But she didn't get to the top because she was Hef's daughter. She got there because she was a respected leader and her own person. Christie always had a sense of who she was and where she was going.

Christie went to Brandeis with the goal of earning a graduate degree in law or journalism. After she graduated, and had gotten some seasoning at the Boston Phoenix, her plan was to apply to Yale's public policy program. But her father intercepted her with an invitation: "On your way to do doing whatever you're going to do, why don't you take a one-year tour through the company?" Christie says, "In hindsight, I think he thought this was a chance for us to spend some time together." The reality is that they both saw it as a short-term assignment.

Divorced from Christie's mother, "Hef" only visited Christie on birthdays and the occasional holiday. Though he wasn't present, his magazine was. "My mother read it, along with *Time, The Atlantic,* and *The New Yorker,*" Christie says. She didn't see her father as the world saw him—the party boy bookended by buxom blondes; she saw her father as a man who published a credible magazine that even her mother read. "My impressions of him were always forged by my sense of him as a person, not an icon. And my attitude toward him was shaped by my mother's very accepting attitude."

It was easy for Christie to accept an invitation from the person, not the icon. "I didn't come into the company as the heir apparent with all the complications and pressure that comes with that. I was likening it to a junior year abroad, an interesting one-year experience." But in that first year Christie saw that Playboy's values were more in line with her own than she previously thought. Her father wanted to use its business success to communicate a sociopolitical agenda centered on personal freedom and civil liberties.

In her early days, Christie worked with *Playboy's* editor in chief to learn the nuts and bolts of putting together a magazine. Later, it was the same editor who gave her some career-shaping advice. "He knew I had been a journalist for a year and he told me, 'Think like a journalist. Get everybody's perspective so you can see things from all sides. Everybody has a valid point of view, and you need to consider them all.' When I became CEO, fostering collaboration was the hallmark of my leadership style."

Christie never imagined her gap year would turn into a deeply passionate commitment to her father's company. "I considered my role to be a steward of a brand, a culture, shareholders and employees, and I had an obligation to serve those masters. I had a long-term and emotional stake in Playboy and its people. They saw that, so they believed in me, supported me, and followed me."

Christie earned the right to lead because she never compromised her convictions to work with her father. She didn't sell herself out. "You can be anointed in title," says Christie, "but true power is given by the people you lead." People follow leaders who are authentic, true to themselves and their life's purpose.

Your Own Way

This is the primary challenge for all leaders: to be authentic and true to one's self. For a successor to do so is complicated. Making one's way when a way has already been established can be more difficult than pioneering something new. To follow in the footsteps of a charismatic leader, successors must earn credibility first with themselves (internal credibility) and then with others (external credibility).

Credibility forms when one develops a realistic sense of what he or she is and is true to that. Self-aware successors accelerate the development of internal credibility because they are able to align their actions with who they want to be. It goes back to the psychological concept of the ideal self (who I aspire to be at my best) and the actual self (who my behaviors show me to be). The first task for the generative successor is to bridge the gap between the actual self and the ideal self. As the gap shrinks, authenticity, self-confidence, and self-esteem increase. The gap widens when people fail to become self-aware, ignore feedback, and protect their ego. A self-aware leader will behave only in ways that match his or her beliefs. Confidence, and hence credibility, follows suit when the leader does what she says she'll do. Credibility can't be borrowed; it must be owned, and originates in the actions that follow from belief. This is what Christie Hefner called "being true to [one's]self"—and this is how a successor begins the ascent to the top.

Earning your way to the top does not start with climbing. It begins with digging down to reality, to the bedrock of one's true identity. The success of *Playboy*—after 50 years it still is the most widely read male publication in the United States—depended on the authenticity of its founder and his daughter doing what they did well. Hugh Hefner was its public face, comfortably and sometimes flamboyantly showcasing the Playboy ethos; his daughter was the face and voice of the company in the corporate environment, boardrooms, investor meetings, and business press. As Christie said of her father's iconic role, "There will be no successor. There's no Mini-Me in the wings."

To get to their own sense of leadership authenticity, successors must push through the myth of a legendary parent and become credible to themselves. For Christie Hefner, this did not happen intentionally. There was no grand design for her to run Playboy, to live up to an icon of America's sexual revolution. But Christie had the ability to bring her father's strengths and weaknesses into focus, and to fill in the gaps of his leadership with her strong analytical skills.

This applied to the mystique that surrounded him and often insulated him from the truth. No one wanted to confront "Hef." Christie's ability to see her father and herself clearly gave her the courage to penetrate "the Hef" mystique. "One of the things that I could bring to the job that might offset my limited experience was a fearlessness about telling my father what I thought was the truth. Even if he might not agree with me, he could at least make informed decisions."

Be Honest with Yourself

Finding the courage to confront your weaknesses and sort through reality, which is often unforgivingly complex, reflects the core challenge of differentiation. To arrive at adulthood is to arrive at an accurate and realistic sense of self. For successors to make their way in a family business requires that they first find the way to authenticity: find out who they really are. For some children, the process is riddled with setbacks because they haven't met some of the basic life cycle challenges outlined in Chapter 2. To overcome this, successors may have to take some of the practical data from their lives, reflect on which challenges of the life cycle needs to be revisited, and shift their behavior and mindset.

The existential questions in this process are "Who am I?" and "Who can I be?" A child living in the shadows of his or her parent will struggle to honestly answer these questions, especially if the parent's plan is for the child to lead the family business, regardless of the child's skills and passion. Adolescents are robbed of the ability to develop self-awareness: to know oneself apart from whom others say they are—to develop their own definition of self. Indeed, the real job of a parent is to help successors stay out of the shadow to give them a sense that they are valued inherently for who they are, to establish a realistic sense of who they are, and what they are passionate about, rather than encouraging them to merely become mirror images of their parent. When parents fail to do this, successors can easily lose their way to the top, tripping on their parent's expectations, rather than forging ahead with what they know to be true about themselves. This is authenticity.

"Eighty percent of success is showing up," says American actor, filmmaker, and comedian Woody Allen. And the most important person to show up to is you. Authenticity is not something we have; it's something we choose. It starts with the courage to show up to ourselves and to take a hard look, not a cursory scan, at our inner selves. This does not happen naturally. We are hardwired for self-deception, and our deception is multilayered. Self-deception conceals from the pretender that fact that he is pretending, which makes the pretense seem all the more authentic. In other words, a person is inauthentic about being inauthentic!

Removing the shroud of self-deception starts by first looking not at who we really are but who we are pretending to be, and realizing that we are not that person. Brene Brown defines authenticity as "being willing to let go of who you think that you should be to be who you really are.... This opens up the possibility for people to authentically connect with you."[1] In short, being yourself encourages others to be themselves around you. Authenticity leads to authentic community. Generative leaders of strong and iconic brands understand that power compounds the need for authenticity because it is more difficult for people to be authentic around power. "You have to work hard to get people to tell you what they really think because the combination of power and family business can be deadly," says Christie Hefner, "because people are working just as hard to figure out what you want them to say."

The pretender is the idealized self that we have nurtured since childhood, often abetted by well-intended parents who tell us we are

[1] Brene Brown, *Daring Greatly: How the Courage to Be Vulnerable Transforms the Way We Live, Love, Parent, and Lead* (New York: Gotham Books, 2012).

good at everything. Idealization saves us from the difficult task of facing reality, providing the illusion of security rather than helping us come to grips with the reality in front of us. There is no family idealization conspiracy theory, of course, but it seems families tend to idealize one another. The trap that parents fall into is the stories they tell themselves about their kids. And the trap that children fall into is that they believe these stories, and carry them into their adulthood. They are mired down by the weight of glorious expectations, afraid to admit that there are some things they simply can't do. As the old saying goes, the truth will set you free; however, you first have to have the courage to allow it to do so.

I Go Blind

To fully step out of the shadow of our parents requires that successors develop a realistic sense of who they are. It demands that they stop trying to become something they aren't. It also includes developing clarity of vision about what is true. This, in part, occurs when we face our blind spots. Blind spots are the things that we might not even know that we don't know. The goal is to reduce your blind spots. The myths we create through idealization are full of them. Everyone has blind spots, even the most iconic leaders. They are unavoidable.

Becoming aware of blind spots, a kind of self-awareness, happens in the latter part of the identity-formation stage. The ability to see blind spots is not intuitive. I guess that's why they are called blind spots. To see a blind spot requires intentionality. Of course, a leader will never be aware of every blind spot, but awareness often creates the decision to look for weakness. It's a matter of constant looking. A car's side-view mirror does no good if the driver does not use it. Glancing at it must become intentional until it becomes habit.

When Kathleen Thurmond succeeded her father as the CEO of Best Washington Uniform Supply, Inc., she quickly had to confront her leadership blind spots in order to gain credibility. Her father had a stroke, and she ascended to the top leadership role. Prior to taking over the family business, Thurmond was a nonprofit executive. In the nonprofit sector, her leadership was tempered with compassion. In corporate America, her compassion came across as soft. She says, "[In social work] I learned [to be] very understanding of someone's circumstances. [You can be compassionate for someone who comes to work] late every day and at the same time, you have to hold the line and say, 'Look, I understand something's going on in your life, but this is unacceptable.' … I had to make tough decisions, and I had to learn to do that."

Blind spots reveal the limitations in one's make-up: One can't be all-seeing and all-knowing. But the bigger problem is pretending to be something one is not. The way to authenticity is first to acknowledge what one doesn't know. One of the most honest statements in life, and the one that is going to help the most in establishing credibility, is to simply say, "I don't know," and then to stop pretending that you do.

Idealization, along with the mythology it perpetuates, has its function. It carries a child to the threshold of growing up. But to mature into a credible leader demands pushing through that which hinders us from crossing the threshold into adulthood. The mythology believed as a child helps to simplify the human experience by accounting for only the good. It is the consistency of the information that matters for a good story, not its completeness. The less you know, the easier it is to fit everything you do know into a coherent pattern. Myths make sense of the world, but they are full of blind spots about who a child's parents are and who the child is. Earning one's way to the top demands that successors take regular looks through the side-view mirror, asking questions such as, "Can I lead this $50 million organization?" "Am I tough enough with the leadership team?" "Do I need to develop a new skill set?"

How Parents Can Help

The most fundamental way that parents can help their child build their internal credibility is through holding them accountable. This means making sure that the children do what they say they are going to do by when they say they will complete it, to the level of quality that can be reasonably expected. Too often in families of wealth, children don't come up against the natural limits and accountabilities that a normal child will; thus, they don't have the same level of accountability. Parents sometimes avoid the hard work of accountability for three primary reasons:

1. They fear the conflict and negative reaction that accountability may bring.

2. They have guilt over the amount of time that they spend on the business and don't want to burden their children anymore.

3. They have a need to be liked by their kids, and to be seen as their child's friend.

While there are many more reasons, holding children accountable is a part of the process of showing them who they actually are in the world. It gives children clear feedback on whether they are living up to their responsibilities, and helps them understand their strengths and weaknesses. Without accountability, there is no credibility.

The need for accountability follows successors into their working life. If there is no accountability in their job, it is much more difficult for successors to develop an accurate sense of who they are and gauge their success. It is important in providing accountability, however, that we avoid our natural tendency to shame individuals when they fail. Promoting healthy accountability involves creating an environment of clarity without shame, and providing specific and measurable goals.[2]

What I most often hear from successors is that it is really hard to get fair, objective feedback. Too often, successors get sugarcoated feedback from people who want to court their favor and support. On the flip side, they get overly harsh feedback from people (often their parents) who don't want to be seen as showing favoritism. Sometimes they don't get feedback at all. It is very hard for a successor to find a strong sense of self if there is no objective feedback and accountability.

One successor tells the story of being pulled over in the small town that is home to his family business. The police officer said, "I can't give you a ticket in this town." The power of his last name robbed him of the accountability and opportunity to learn.

Building Belief in Others

Being credible to oneself is only one part of the story. To truly be an effective and generative leader, one must be able to instill a belief in others—develop followers. Developing external credibility involves

---

[2]R.M. Kantor, "Four Tips for Building Accountability," *Harvard Business Review* (August 2009).

establishing objective evidence of competency and building a track record of success. But that is not all. It also requires successors to develop a sense of connection with those whom they are leading. These people need to feel connected to the successor, sensing empathy for their struggles and an understanding of who they are. The biggest sign of external credibility is developing followers.

Daniel Goleman, creator of the concept of emotional intelligence, talks about this as one of three key areas of focus for leaders. Through a focus on understanding how the other thinks and feels, the leader increases the ability to persuade and influence those he is leading.[3]

Internal and external credibility don't exist in isolation. In fact, they most often feed each other. When others express their belief in the successor, it feeds the successor's belief in herself (internal credibility). Likewise, when a successor feels credible to himself, it increases others' belief in the successor as a leader (external credibility).

Building Resiliency

To be authentic is not only to recognize shortcomings. Authenticity means owning it and then telling it. To avoid reality is to pretend it does not exist, and if it doesn't exist, then nothing happened and there is nothing to tell. Strong leaders can accurately describe reality without shaming or playing the role of victim. There is a saying that the chief of the tribe is always the best storyteller. The best storyteller is the one who tells his own story because he owns the narrative and his actions in it. This is taking personal responsibility: telling the whole story, the glorious rise as well as the inglorious fall.

To assume this kind of responsibility is a paramount leadership task.

John Tyson, the CEO of Tyson Foods, Inc., is point blank in how he describes and owns his failure. "I'm a recovering alcoholic and drug addict. It's a personal failure. It's a form of responsibility to myself and to those who are counting on me. My addiction sidelined me, but I went and recovered. I had to reestablish my credibility, to myself first. And after that, I just worked. The day I reestablished my

---

[3]Daniel Goleman, *Focus: The Hidden Driver of Excellence* (New York: Harper Collins, 2013).

credibility to the people in my company was the day I was offered the CEO job." Embracing his failures was a crucial step toward assuming the larger responsibility of leading and caring for thousands of employees. "There is a tremendous set of obligations that goes along with leading a company, a tremendous set of responsibilities and personal sacrifices," says Tyson. "It starts with choices. People are afraid of choices." Tyson knows the fear of taking responsibility for those choices, as well as the strength a person finds when he does.

Parents who indulge their children often forsake teaching their children responsibility. At some point, parents can no longer kiss their children's hurt to make it better. Instead, they must teach their children to identify the problem and solve it. It also includes giving the gift of resiliency—the ability to soldier toward a goal through obstacles and failure. One of the ways that parents do this is to hold their children accountable.

Resiliency is born from credibility. In family-run businesses, it comes less from being a family member, and more from who you are and how you show up. Trek Bicycle's founder, Richard Burke, took an "earn it" approach with his son, John. Richard never presumed John would take over for him some day. He neither subtly pushed the business on him nor blatantly told him he would inherit the business. All he did was leave the door open. "If you're interested," he told John, "you can get a job at Trek. Your last name will get you in the door and the rest is up to you." John Tyson, who started working on his father's chicken farm at the age of 13, reflects the same philosophy of family business succession: "It's your life. It's not your parents' life, not the coach's life, not the pastor's life. It's your life. I don't think it's our job to help them find [the right place]. Our job is to simply give them permission."

A large part of developing resiliency is stripping illusions of dependency that keep one from authenticity. If a parent refuses to swoop in and rescue a child encountering hardship, that child will begin to look inward for the resources to deal with life's challenges. This is the school of hard knocks, one of the most important lessons of self-education. Parents help in that process by giving their children the privilege of working and the freedom to make mistakes, to learn from their failure as well as their success. Work, real work, helps potential successors learn what they are capable of while also revealing what they aren't capable of when they run up against the hard stop of human limitations. Work reveals reality.

It is for this reason that problems often crop up when predecessors (often parents) prematurely vault their child into senior-level leadership. Without credible work experience, a successor is stuck in the myth that he or she is capable by virtue of name alone, not by way of skills, experience, and passion. Sheltering children from their inevitable failure, the predecessor swoops in, solves the problem, and hence, reinforces the predecessor-hero myth. Sometimes predecessors unconsciously place a successor in a role in which they'll fail, so they can be the save-the-day hero. Regardless of intentionality, a family member who is prematurely placed in leadership will more often struggle to establish external credibility because he or she does not have the skill sets or track record to succeed. For example, if a family member is handed a role that requires leading seasoned professionals, and the leader is perceived as paralyzed by hard decisions, he or she will not be respected by the other executives.

Some predecessors simply don't know when a successor is ready to lead. The stories of my research reveal, however, that the most seamless transitions from founder to successor happen when parents soberly answer several questions:

- Are my successor's skill sets increasing?
- Is my successor becoming technically capable?
- Is there a track record of success?
- Has my successor developed followers?
- Is my successor aware of personal blind spots?
- Is my successor being authentic, or is it pretense?
- Is my successor passionate about what he or she is doing?
- Is there objective data to support an increase in responsibility?

The alternate scenario is that some successors recognize they are ready before their parents do. And many are. If a family succession plan is in place, a successor must be patient and work through existing structures. This is complicated for successors, however, who often aren't promoted as quickly as their credibility develops. In these situations, often the only solution is to look outside the organization. In fact, Bill Wrigley was in discussions with a board member about the possibility of leaving the company when his father fell ill. Because he saw himself as credible and felt he needed the opportunity for growth, he said to himself, *if I can't grow inside the family company, I will find a place where I can.*

Show Up for Work

"The only successors here at Tyson Foods," says John Tyson, "would be those who worked hard and got a chance to do more." Successors with credibility earn their way to the top as they immerse themselves in the work of the family business. Successors construct a framework of authenticity and credibility upon a foundational triad of self-awareness, skill, and passion. They do not develop self-awareness through mere introspection, of course. It happens as they test who they are through the discipline of hard work, discovering their skills, and passions. A theme that runs through all my research is that as successors learn to work, they simultaneously learn about themselves.

Earlier in this chapter, I wrote about the gap between who a person thinks she is and who she really is. Work not only serves to expose the gap; work also helps to bridge the gap. To the extent that there are gaps, a successor brings them into the workplace and asks: What values do I stand for?

- Are there gaps between my values and how I actually behave?
- What impact do I want to have in my life and my career?
- What are my skills and talents?
- What does the feedback that I get tell me about my performance?
- Is there a gap between the talent and skills I have today and those that I will need going forward?

And, of course, to succeed in a family business, the leader doesn't work for the sake of work. The leader works for the sake of meaning; for the livelihood of those dependent on the business for their livelihood; and for the joy of building something great, which unites everyone around a common purpose. To lead means to inspire. And to emerge as a generative leader, a successor asks him- or herself a third question: How should I align the values, vision, and action in a way that affects the people I am leading? That's passion. One gains the skill set and stokes the inner fire of passion through meaningful work experience. Work establishes a successor's track record—it is data by which a successor can measure his or her true ability; identify blind spots; and develop a plan to keep learning to establish and maintain credibility.

That experience rarely begins with what many think of as passion. Working one's way to the top does not start with an attitude of naïve entitlement and the expectation of euphoric engagement in a dream job. It might start with work that a potential successor hates (the assembly line floor) and learns to enjoy. It involves trying different things and learning through action.

The summer before his sophomore year in college, John Burke worked the graveyard shift at a plastics factory making "Season's Greetings" plastic candy-cane molds filled with M&Ms. He hated it. John shucked out plastic candy-cane molds all night, wearing gloves with holes that burned his hands. One morning, as he sat eating breakfast alone, his father came into the kitchen.

"How was work?"

"Terrible, it was just the worst," John said, hoping for a bit of commiseration. "I'm not going back. I'll look for something else."

"You'll go back and you'll enjoy the job, and it will be a great experience."

His father then walked out the door. Of that summer job, John says, "It turned out to be one of the great work experiences of my life."

Richard Burke taught his son a valuable lesson. And it wasn't simply the value of hard work or the truism that if you work at something long enough you will learn something from it. Rather, it was if you bring yourself to work and invest yourself in it, you will begin to develop a sense of yourself. Work matters because of what you bring to it, being fully present in it. To be all there. His father's confident assertion, "You'll go back," instilled in John an approach to work that now galvanizes the entire Trek organization. "One of the things I like to say, 'It's another great day to be working at the best bicycle company in the world.' "

Skills and passion can follow attitude, as they did for John when at the age of 24, his father put him in charge of sales and marketing for Trek Bicycle Corporation. Too restless to get good grades as a history major at Boston University, John was drawn to a business course where he won top prize for developing a business plan, which he quickly developed into a business. But his father's force field pulled strongly. John went to work at Trek, and one year after college became Trek's top sales rep. While out selling, John was also listening to the customers rag on his father's company. "There is no greater learning experience," John said, "then getting your head kicked in listening to how bad the family business is." John absorbed the beating and channeled what he learned into turning customer service around. John had the right stuff for leadership: an innate entrepreneurial sense, quick development of skills in the field, and a relentless positive response to customer complaints.

John earned the inner credibility to take on the mantle of leadership in his father's company. He didn't do so by being Dick Burke's kid. He showed up for work, seizing every opportunity, good and bad.

But he also got to the top because he was credible—not just the icon's son. His father sparked the fire of passion the day he said, "You'll go back to work … " John only did so because he had learned to listen to his dad and to take his advice. Listening itself was another skill John learned from his father. "Nobody does a better job than Trek in listening to its customers. The ability to listen to your customers and not have it bother you, that was my dad," John says.

The strength of their relationship enabled the two to go at it. They often disagreed over business decisions, sometimes leading to heated discussions when the business was suffering. Fierce confrontations often arise out of fierce bonds of friendship. Resistance strengthens a relationship or a business when the friendship or partnership is strong. The bond was strengthened by the rigorous activities they did together. "I ran three Boston marathons with him," John says, "and I hate running."

This theme surfaces throughout interviews I conducted: A successor rises to the top most often when the child feels credible to him- or herself, is respected by parents, and has the support of those being led.

John Burke's story of ascent, like Christie Hefner's, illustrates the axiom that the whole is greater than the sum of its parts. In establishing the legacy of a family business, the relationship of founder and successor must be mutually respectful. Both Playboy and Trek became stronger companies when both parent and child led them together. Too often, the founder's legend undermines the credibility of a successor, so powerful and so dominating that it not only overshadows but also disables the adult child, who remains stymied forever in a teenage psyche. John Burke and Christie Hefner were able to make their way by building an enduring internal framework of self-awareness, skill, and passion. In doing so, they did not just perpetuate the myth of their legendary parents, they wrote compelling stories of their own for the next chapter in the family business. And they continued to build on their family's legacy and abiding values.

"This company does great things for people, many of which people never see," John says. "We're here for a much bigger reason than just making money. That came from my parents. Nobody else." And it comes now from their son.

John Burke knows whom he follows, but he has never followed his father blindly. Perhaps it's summed up best in the way John Burke describes his father, with a mixture of admiration and understanding: "He's a legend. That's just the way he is. Cut him some slack."

ENTITLEMENT

One of the most common fears that I hear from parents in family business is the fear that our children will feel entitled and will squander the family fortune. In fact, our society often reflects that fear by portraying successors as unqualified and arrogant. This stereotype overlooks the vast majority of successors who are hardworking, caring, and committed professionals. Generally, people are more drawn to the stories about *trust-fund babies* who squander their fortune, treat others with disdain, and exhibit a sense that they are better than anyone else.

While there are certainly successors that fit this stereotype, my 20 years of experience with family businesses says that most successors are competent and committed. So how can one work to avoid inculcating a sense of entitlement in the next generation?

To deal with entitlement, we must first understand its origins. Entitlement blossoms from a sense of inadequacy and vulnerability. Successors who exhibit a sense of entitlement often have a sense of vulnerability that stems from feeling that they aren't worthy of love and they aren't valuable on their own. They develop the sense that in order to be loved and valuable in this family and in the world, I have to show my money, have a lot of things, or assert my name or position as the source of my authority. I am not valuable just because of who I am and who my actions show me to be.

The shadow created by the myths of our predecessors can create this sense that I am not enough on my own, that I can't possibly live up to what has gone before.

To prevent a sense of entitlement, parents must move beyond the common mistakes that can contribute to an attitude of entitlement in the next generation:

- Setting a bad example. Kids learn from the example that their parents set. If their parents exhibit an attitude of entitlement or don't teach a connection between actions and consequences, it is unlikely that the next generation will learn a sense of responsibility.

- Lack of accountability. Often, the growing wealth of a family creates an environment where children aren't held accountable for their actions. If children get whatever they want by asking, and are never shown a model that connects hard work with reward and delayed gratification, they will not feel a sense of pride or ownership in earning what they have. In addition, if parents don't want to deal with the drama of disciplining children because it makes them feel uncomfortable, they will prevent their children from learning the connection between actions and consequences.

- Trying to be your child's best friend. The motivation to be your child's friend is based on the parent's need to be loved and receive the adoration of the child. It ignores the real role of a parent—to provide structure, predictability, and an environment where children can learn and experience life while being protected from catastrophic injury.

4

The Strength of Failure

Running the obstacle course of success

It may have been his father's birthday, but Mike Hamra received all the attention.

On January 1, 2011, during the celebration of his 79th birthday, Sam Hamra of Hamra Enterprises publicly handed over leadership of his company to Mike. The media called it a surprise announcement.

But for Mike it was anticlimactic. Just a few years earlier, Mike says, "I woke up one morning and told myself that I was going to be in charge." Mike walked into his father's office and announced, "Your right-hand guy … I'm going to fire him next week. And some of the people around him, they're off the bus, too. They aren't good for us, Dad." And his dad agreed.

In retrospect, Mike realizes that pushing was perhaps the only way to succeed his father, who did not want let go of the company. "The business was his life, and he wanted to be in charge until the day he died." The business helped his father manage meaning in this life.

"But when I came in to fire his number one guy, my dad knew that I was ready, and so was he. He realized, 'Mike's got it. I can step away.'"

Although Sam did little to expedite his son's rise to the top of the company, he always hoped his son would take over. "My dad did not have a succession plan," Mike says. "He gave me no clear pathway in the business that included a timeline. All he did early on was convince me *not* to follow my dream to be a jet fighter pilot. He pointed me in a different direction, changed the trajectory of my life, and let me do the rest."

Mike made his own way to the top of Hamra Enterprises.

He started the rise in an unlikely place: an elevator on Capitol Hill. Mike was its operator. At law school Mike had no interest in business, and decided to make a career of public service in Washington, DC. But the only job he could find was operating the elevator for the Senate Sergeant of Arms Office for $16,000 a year. Though starting at the bottom, Mike was undeterred. He found the confined space a good place to network with a captive audience. When he met Senator John Glenn on the elevator one evening, Mike asked him for advice on how to find meaningful work in DC. The next morning, Mike was on the phone with the Senator's Administrative Assistant, who then helped Mike in finding a political job in DC, That brief encounter in the elevator eventually led to a job working for Kansas City Congresswoman Karen McCarthy.

Mike quickly leveraged his new connections to land an appointment in the Clinton administration as special assistant to the chief of staff to the National Telecommunications and Information Administration (NTIA), which is hosted at the US Department of Commerce. From there, his jobs became increasingly significant and challenging, culminating in an interoperability project for the NTIA. Mike's work helped national and local safety agencies coordinate efforts and save lives during the 9/11 attack.

After his stint in the Clinton Administration, Mike landed a job at the Federal Communications Commission (FCC). Mike credits his political experience as the training ground for his business success. Mike learned how to manage people, especially when it came to making connections with employees. "Our deputy chief of staff at the FCC was a sphinx," says Mike. "No one could connect with him when he was in his office, so I needed to find another angle to connect because I needed his focus in order to get things done. That was when I figured out that he was going outside three times a day to have a cigarette, and I figured it was the only time he might relax and let his guard down. So I joined him three times a day and got invaluable information from him and get the things that I needed handled."

At the age of 25, as chief of staff to an FCC wireless bureau chief, Mike was tasked with reducing a three-year backlog of processing wireless licenses, and to maneuver through a labyrinth of rules and regulations surrounding the process. When he didn't move things along fast enough, Mike lost his job as the Chief of Staff but stayed at the FCC.

"It's tough to get fired from a government job," Mike laughs, "but I managed to do it. Getting canned was a good learning experience."

Mike gleaned valuable lessons from his experiences in government leadership. Inertia, for instance, was more a management problem than a bureaucratic inevitability. "The challenge in government is to hold people accountable when there is no real threat of losing their jobs. I tried to be nice instead of holding people accountable. I realized you can't get people moving by being nice. It fosters a culture of inertia and excuses. When people are excusing their bad behavior, they aren't learning and growing."

In an often-disingenuous environment, Mike learned the value of being straightforward. After being fired, he became a legal writer for the FCC, and worked one of the most complex rule makings in the wireless bureau. Part of the job was freeing up a mobile radio band for Nextel Communications. "The other owners of licenses in the band didn't like it," Mike says. "But I knew that what they wanted was authenticity, straight talk about what was going on. So I met with their coalition for two days and told them what we were doing, that they weren't going to like it, but that we weren't going to let complaints run the show. For that, I won a lot of respect."

By 1997, Mike wanted to earn more than respect. He needed to make money. He left the FCC for a private law firm, where he made enough money to buy a home and sharpen his skills as a researcher and writer. But Mike found private practice too restrictive to accommodate his larger political ambition. "I loved Washington, DC, its politics and diversity, its global-impact, high-profile work that actually made a difference in the world."

Capitalizing on his experience with the FCC, Mike joined a start-up company called Metricom, a joint venture between Paul Allen and MCI WorldCom. Metricom made him the director of government and regulatory affairs, a job that he loved, until the company declared bankruptcy—within six months of Mike's hiring date. But in that brief time, Mike got what he needed: a passion for business and a realization that the private sector could also serve the greater good. Mike stayed on another six months to help liquidate the company. That's when his father came calling.

And Mike was ready.

Developing Gut Instincts: Learning through Action

Mike Hamra traveled the bumpy road of success and failure during his early career in Washington, DC—and wasn't derailed. When he was fired, he did not quit. He learned.

Leaders like Hamra develop an instinct to lead from the painful but rewarding process of trying out new things, making mistakes, and learning from them. Experience—not only gained through action but guided by personal values—leads to improved intuition. When he got his paycheck from the FCC, Mike Hamra learned the value of accountability in a political culture that did not reinforce it. Good leaders see what others often fail to learn—what it is they value. Such self-awareness and subsequent self-confidence can help successors find the lesson in their failures rather than seeking sources for blame, as is our natural tendency.

Mike had proved his strength as a leader outside of the business, but he still needed to gain credibility within Hamra Enterprises. When Mike joined his father's company, Sam Hamra had just gotten into Panera Bread in the Chicago market. He asked Mike to help with the development of the Chicago market and a new market to be developed in Boston. When Mike saw that Hamra's first partner in Boston was mismanaging the operation, Mike fired him. A lack of accountability, accompanied by a tolerance of mediocrity, was unacceptable.

One of the marks of a leader is the ability to make hard decisions, like firing marginal employees. Letting go of incompetent employees in key positions, Mike trusted his gut instincts. His cumulative work experience, including being fired from the FCC job, helped to understand the importance of accountability and to develop the self-confidence to make difficult judgment calls on a company's most valuable resource: its employees. Fire mediocrity; hire competency.

The only way a leader can develop the instinct to make the tough (and right) calls is through the painful but instructive process of taking action. To engage the world and learn from the experience involves taking action and making mistakes. These are often painful. A child learns that the stove is dangerous by touching it when it's hot.

Pain, born from experience, is a good data source. The accumulated lessons form a leader's intuition. This is the gut feeling that he or she learns to pay attention to and to trust.

The creation and formation of the gut of a leader is shaped by learning that can only come through taking action, the trauma of mistakes, and the layers of accumulated experience that leads to expertise. The more experiences, the greater the leader's awareness of his strengths that helps him trust his instincts. At the same time, they are conscious that their intuition can sometimes produce biases, and they use self-awareness to pair their gut with the data to make the right decisions. Self-awareness demands pushing against the world, finding out what works, taking chances, and being accountable for the outcome.

Hamra's values guided his gut—and his decisiveness.

The Hard Road to Leadership

The leaders we have studied thus far emerged from the shadows of the family mythology to write their own stories, with themselves as the owners of the narrative. To do so, they had to establish their own identity apart from their parents. This is differentiation, which I spoke about in Chapter 2.

Successors falter when dysfunctional family patterns make it difficult to pursue differentiation. These include mental illness, addictions, family trauma, and personality disorders. Dealing with these may require professional intervention. All the qualities we have looked at so far in emerging successors of family businesses point to an ability to deal with family dysfunction and integrate family values and tradition with their own values and convictions.

A family business becomes stronger through the generations as children learn to leave their parents without leaving them behind. Dealing with the family's hard stuff so the stuff of the family business can be dealt with. Successors must develop the strength to perpetuate the family legacy while separating from the family (and its dysfunction) so they can lead the business. In a family business, this requires a shift in the relationship, from doing what their parents want, to start doing what *they* think is right for the family and the business. And understanding that what they want is an extension of who they are, and how they can uniquely contribute to the world. This revelation rarely manifests as a magical "aha" moment, but through a process of failing, learning through action, trusting their gut, learning what one likes and dislikes, and continually assessing the gap between goals and outcomes.

This is how a successor develops intuition, to trust what's right. Living in the shadow of the myth, successors are told what's right or they pursue their interpretation of what their parents think is right. But credibility is earned by actually experiencing what is right, rather than taking someone's word for it, and by building a track record of success through action. Parents have a set of experiences that have led to their gut instinct about what to do in certain situations. Because of the era in which they lived, their experiences and failures, their personality, their economic status—this gut instinct worked for them. But successors must come to realize that they are different persons, in a different time, with a different context.

Many successors are so mired in the past they can't get to where they want to go. Successors must develop their own gut instinct. When I counsel family businesses, I remind them that they are always in this constant equation of, "What do I need to hold onto about the past and nurture, and use as meaning-making and a foundation, and what do I need to let go of and change to move forward?" You hone your decision-making capacity through action.

No Mistakes; Just Learning

Despite the lasting stereotypes of the Silver Spoon Club, the vast majority of children of successful and wealthy parents tend to succeed, whatever they choose to do. But the harder road to success might be committing to the family business. For some, that commitment will demand a sacrifice of self: an abandonment of professional and (sometimes) personal pursuits. It is a vow of loyalty, a covenant to the ongoing success of the family (not merely the business). Bella Hoare of C. Hoare & Co. gives this piece of advice: "Don't join until you're damn sure you want to stay there. It's worse than getting married and then getting divorced. Lots of people get divorced; it doesn't mean you're a bad person. But leaving your family business makes you almost unemployable. So don't slide into working there by mistake. Make a conscious decision."

Erma Bombeck once referred to "The family ties that bind and gag." In family business, to bind the family, rather than gagging it, means that children have to gain a measure of independence from their family of origin. As we have discussed, they have to become their own persons. Successors like Bella Hoare and Mike Hamra achieved success within the family only after assuring they were ready to do so. They developed their leadership and business acumen far away from their families. This is when trial and error taught them what they liked, were skilled at, and would most naturally succeed at.

Living in the shadow of the myth makes it more difficult for successors to find their identity. Their identity tends to be inseparable from the business and, therefore, to the myth of the founder or predecessor. They come into leadership not because of experience but because of name. As Dick DeVos said, "Sometimes people are born on third base and the problem is they think they hit a triple."

Credibility is hitting a triple, which demands practice, persistence through the slumps, and tweaking one's form. Successors in family businesses must get to the point where they have developed the internal credibility to say to their predecessors, "I can be successful with or without you, and I choose to be successful with you."

That's not to say that successors have to leave to lead. Yes, the general rule is that it's easier to differentiate if you're not ingrained in the everyday life of your family. But the myth is that outside work experience is the only way to differentiate. There are exceptions all the time. It's not a death knell if a leader doesn't get outside work experiences. There are those whose passion overcomes the obstacles of differentiation within the context of the family business. They figure out a way to fill in the gaps of inexperience. In the trenches, they try out multiple jobs in the organization; they seek a secondary education, like an MBA; they find a mentor; they sign on for executive coaching; or they join a professional network. Simply, they find the tools to develop while remaining open to the lessons learned on the job.

This was the case for Jean Moran, who says that she "pretty much went to school within the business." Jean transformed her father's company, Label Makers Inc., into LMI Packaging Solutions, a leader in the flexible packaging industry. Jean's father, Chester Sykes, started the company in the back of a Chicago butcher shop after he was laid off for secretly building a press in a garage. Chester would do anything to have his own company. His mission statement, "a place where his employees will always have a voice," was a reaction to the company he had worked for, whose ownership muzzled its employees.

Chester was self-taught, "a genius who didn't finish high school and could fix anything." Of her own bachelor's degree in recreation Jean says, "Everybody gives their condolences, until I tell them that the entire curriculum was based on Murphy's law, that if anything can go wrong it will. Like, "You're planning a picnic for 3,000 kids, and it rains. What do you do?" It's just like business." Jean shares her father's propensity to take away vital lessons from every learning experience, especially when things go wrong. "There are no mistakes," she says, "there's just learning."

Jean tested her philosophy early on, when she was working part-time for the company, and made one of her biggest "non-mistakes," a perfect example of Murphy's law in action. "I didn't know anything," she says, "and a supplier calls me and says, 'The price is going up on your material, but if you order today, you'll save $30,000; if you wait until the day we are scheduled to deliver, it will cost you $30,000.' This was a no-brainer, I thought. Send the material. The next day five semi-trucks show up on our little neighborhood street, blocking all the traffic, including me in my car, and I say, 'What the hell is going on!'"

Not only was she clueless about what was going on, she was also clueless that she was responsible. She had no place for the material and no cash to fund it. That's the day she learned her first of many lessons from Professor Failure: "When you screw up, the best thing to do is just keep going." Strong leaders are good learners who get top grades in the subject of failure. When a long line of trucks arrived with the material, there was no place to put the trucks or the materials. Jean had to get people to move their cars in the parking lot, and shift materials in the warehouse and the office to make room for all this material. Jean said, "We had skids of material everywhere, for months. I cringe in thinking about it again."

One successor (let's call him John) tells the story of the challenge of dealing with failure. A member of his senior leadership team had just made a mistake that had cost the company $3 million. John called this individual into his office and asked him if he knew why he was there. The individual said, "You're going to fire me." To the man's surprise, John said, "I just gave you a $3 million education. Why would I fire you? And let someone else take advantage of that learning?"

Optimistic leaders like Jean Moran understand that when they fail, they have also learned something, and they view obstacles as opportunities to make corrections or to innovate. They overcome failure and build self-esteem by persevering through repeated attempts at getting it right. This perseverance brings their actual selves into alignment with their ideal selves.

Jean's ascent to leadership is a case study of learning by trial and error, starting with what she didn't know, and persevering until she had it down. "My dad and I were very close," Jean says. "I would have done anything for him, and when I took over the business, my dad knew something that I didn't yet know: there was no way I was going to let this thing fail."

Jean's learning curve was not steep so much as it was relentless and steady. Her trajectory looks like a primer in perseverance: continuing education, a CPA degree, leadership coaching, a leadership development program run by Vistage, mentors, family counseling, asking for help from anyone who knew more than she did. It also included taking calculated risks, like losing big clients to gain more profitable ones.

Supporting Failure

Children begin to get a sense of their capacities and limitations as they start to explore their world and test themselves against it. Some personalities gravitate to challenging environments—difficult and demanding situations that call for risk; they are willing to learn by failing at something that exceeds their capacity. These are the kids who always want more. Children who are risk takers want to run before they can walk. They thrive on the challenge, and eventually rise to it, even if they break a few bones on the way.

With children who may not be natural risk takers, parents may encourage them to take risks by, simply, not demonizing their children's failure. In wealthy and successful families, children who rise to leadership learn early on that risk can bring reward. Their parents encourage the process by giving successors opportunity for failure, as long as the failure doesn't threaten to sink the ship. In these families, failure is not a deterrent.

I have explored the mythologies surrounding family success, and how difficult it is for successors to emerge from the shadow of legendary predecessors. But some families also perpetuate a mythology of failure, a mindset that inhibits risk. Nick Perrino carried such a mythology into his business. When he told his son Joe, "With your stupid ideas, six months after I die you're going to blow up this business," that was fear talking. Joe Perrino's ideas were neither stupid nor would they blow up the business. In fact, they grew Home Run Inn exponentially.

Fear drives a mythology of failure because it is a perception based on prior experience that precludes the possibility of success. Past failure may mean a family filters what's new through the lens of fear. Nick Perrino interpreted Joe's innovation as an impending apocalypse because Nick had experienced his world falling apart. As a result, his approach was always cautious: "Let's protect ourselves." Joe, however, saw opportunity, emerged from that fear-based mythology, and wrote a new story of success.

Some successors use reflection to push through the fear. Others need reinforcement from the community that they aren't getting from their parents or predecessor. One would think that the barrage of negativity from his father would have caused Joe to shy away from risk. No doubt, Joe's naturally more positive personality contributed to decisions. But Joe also received positive feedback from his community, who praised him for his leadership on the baseball diamond. A successor gains an accurate sense of who he or she is through self-reflection, parental reinforcement, and environmental factors. When failure becomes shameful and stigmatized, the culture of the system begins to discourage measured risk taking that is important to the growth and development of the company.

When feedback mechanisms fail, a mythology of failure may be internalized. The successor is more prone to perceive him- or herself as a failure. One job of parenting is to prevent children from identifying themselves by their mistakes. Instead, they must encourage (even celebrate) failure, because this is how strength is built. When parents encourage their children to explore and experiment, they are also preparing children to be comfortable with failure. Failure is not only an option; it is a likely outcome. When children are free to blaze trails and let ideas fly, failure can be one of the guideposts along the way to success. We need to let successors experience failures, but failures that won't sink the ship.

For parents to help successors fail well, they need to help their children identify their mistakes, and understand them, and to move beyond a culture of blame and shame, developing the understanding that failure happens.[1]

Bob Vermeer, chairman emeritus of Vermeer Corporation, talked about how his father helped him deal with failure. Bob shared, "The one thing that I always appreciated [about my dad] is that he didn't seem to hold a grudge [when you failed]. He always looked at it and asked what you learned from the experience and moved on. It needed to be acknowledged, but then you moved on."

Failure can be a badge of honor instead of a mark of shame, like a scar that tells a story of a daring feat that didn't quite go right. But there was the courageous attempt. A parent supports the effort, encouraging children to continue to stay engaged with the world to learn from the actions that they have taken. Shame discourages engagement. Shame promotes withdrawal: to pull up, pull back, to avoid failure. The goal becomes to not fail instead of trying to achieve a goal.

When Jean Moran's father told his daughter to figure it out, he was also giving her the permission to make mistakes. What Jean internalized was the audacious idea that there are no mistakes, only learning. Successors learn by taking action through the encouragement of their parents. Richard Branson said in an interview that his mom had no qualms about dropping him off three miles from home and saying, "Find your way back." He said in the interview, "I made it home safe and sound, but that wasn't the only time Mum put me to the test. When I was 12, she had me cycle 50 miles to a relative's house all by myself. … Going through with these feats was anything but easy, but it forced me to experience the world on my own."[2] What some would say bordered on bad parenting, he interpreted as extreme confidence in his ability to do what he needed to do. It set him up later in life to possess extreme confidence.

Exposure to failure also encourages the development of self-awareness, a leadership trait that I have stressed throughout this book. Parents who expose their children to failure do not say to them, "Suck it up; it builds character." Instead, they will ask their

---

[1] M. McCardle, *The Upside of Down: Why Failing Well is the Key to Success* (New York: Viking: The Penguin Group, 2014).

[2] R. Branson, "Richard Branson on the Importance of Independence," *Entrepreneurship* (August 18, 2014), http://www.entrepreneur.com/article/236178.

kids, "What did you learn?" So the children can reflect on what the failure has taught them. When I asked one CEO, "What did your parents do that made you successful?" she said, "Whenever I failed, my dad said, 'Good job! What did you learn?'" It's about creating a context for failure in the midst of a mythology of success. If failure is not allowed, if success is the only reality, children will find it difficult to step out of the shadow of their legendary parents. What they will internalize is that they can't possibly live up to the legends that preceded them.

Obstacle Courses

Parents who teach their children to deal with failure do more than just passively allow their kids free run of the farm or the forest. They also place thoughtful challenges (obstacles) in their pathway. Just as brain teasers build the cerebral cortex, obstacle courses build tenacity. Playgrounds can be set up as obstacle courses for children. Play can present great opportunity for children to learn limitations by pushing their boundaries. Hanna Rosin's article "The Overprotected Kid" explores the merits of a new adventure playground in England, called the Land.[3] Daring conventional wisdom about play (and the peace of parents), the Land looks more like a dump than a schoolyard playground. There isn't a child-safe plastic slide, swing, or tic-tac-toe board in sight. Instead, there's a frayed rope that swings a child over a creek; a barrel in which children can create a fire; rough-edged pallets for building; a pile of tires for climbing; and discarded mattresses upon which to bounce. Rosin writes: "The idea was that kids should face what to them seems like 'really dangerous risks' and then conquer them alone. That ... is what builds self-confidence and courage."

When risk, pain, and struggle are scrubbed from life, the chance to discover meaning and to overcome challenges that create self-esteem is lost. It's that process of meeting challenges through which children develop internal credibility.

Consistency is the hallmark of this kind of challenging parenting. Children who are challenged one day and indulged the next learn only to try to work the system to get reward and avoid punishment. They may not internalize the value of their actions until they

---

[3] Hanna Rosin, "The Overprotected Kid," *The Atlantic* (April 2014).

are allowed to live with the consequences. Parents in wealthy families often opt out of the task of consistently challenging their children and holding them accountabile, preferring instead the way of indulgence. A parent who struggles to put food on the table can easily say, "No, you can't have a PlayStation." A wealthy parent has the means to do both, and must decide whether or not to say no. This is what can help children understand the difference between need and want.

The Family Launching Pad: Go Out and Get It

Scientists and engineers do not build a rocket to admire it, as it sits on the launching pad. Mission control's most exciting moment is the launch sequence. The family is ground zero for a successor's development and growth into a leader. All the family resources are focused on that defining moment when the girders fall away and the child launches.

In this new phase of life, it's critical that the emerging leader develop his or her own support system. Most critical is the feedback loop and the establishment of accountability. These lead to the emotional intelligence and stability that a successor will need to guide and stabilize a business through inevitable transition and change.

A self-appointed accountability system is especially important for children of wealth. Those with a wealth of resources, money, intelligence, and tremendous capacity have fewer natural obstacles. They travel life's highways with fewer traffic jams. They often can become blind to their own faults. No matter how good a leader is, it's peers who decide how far he or she goes. The emerging leader learns to check his or her emotions against reality, coming to terms with truth that people have baggage.

The Shape of Success

"Unless we get something worked out, I am leaving, because this is not going to work for me." Mike Hamra had succeeded beyond his expectations but at a great price: a bitter impasse with his father.

Mike had done everything necessary to turn Hamra Enterprises around. He had reduced debt, made its companies more profitable, and, more importantly, changed the company culture by seeking more input from employees. The company was energized from its base. But one thing was missing. Mike had not involved his father. As the company thrived, the father–son relationship had deteriorated.

"The situation was toxic," and the only solution, Mike thought, was for him to leave.

And then something shifted for Mike. "All this time, I had seen it as a competition of control of the company. But I realized all my dad wanted was to feel involved … that he could still make it happen. He had based his identity on being CEO." Simply, Mike had become more self-aware.

"I discovered a personal development program," Mike explains. "It helped me to be present to myself, and how I showed up to others. If you want to effect change, the shift has to first be internal. You have to shift your own view and how you hear what others are saying. You need to let go of your filters that cloud your listening." Mike eyes were opened to the needs of his father.

Leading Hamra Enterprises was an education, just as Mike's previous work experience was. Amidst his success at turning around the company, Mike was forced to confront his errors in dealing with his father. In many ways, the business only truly began to thrive when the father–son, predecessor–successor relationship was salvaged. It began when Mike answered, "How do I develop a healthy relationship [with my father]?"

He already learned to listen to his employees, a skill he adopted because of his previous work experience. Now he needed to listen to his father.

"I realized there was no winning in telling him that he needed to step out of the business. That was a dead end." All Sam Hamra needed was for his son to understand his fear of giving up his life's work.

"After several years of my leadership," Mike says, "it became clear to my dad that he needed to give up the CEO position. So when I actually walked in and said, 'You are gonna give it up,' he said, 'I know.'"

Working through the myth that only one leader could be "the" legend allowed both mortals to work toward the future of the family enterprise.

OUTSIDE WORK EXPERIENCE

For many years, the prevailing wisdom of family business consultants has been to advise family businesses to have their children work outside the family business for a period of time. This advice is typically given with the following rationale:

- They can learn what it is like to work for someone else.

- They can make mistakes in a neutral environment where those mistakes won't follow them their entire career.

- They can build valuable skill sets and knowledge from other organizations that can help their family business.

- They can learn to support themselves financially.

Karl-Erivan Haub, CEO of Tengelmann, shares a personal story regarding the value of his outside work experience at Nestlé. "The best part was that they gave me a car and 96 stores in the San Francisco area, which I had to service for three months. They didn't know who I was. They didn't care who I was. So I had to sell products, displays, shelf levels, and pricing—especially with independent grocers. This was super because I realized that I can do that. That gave me the confidence that even if I wouldn't be in the [family] company, I would always be able to survive. I knew from that point on."

This concept is based on the idea that it will be easier for the successor to differentiate from their parents and their family when they are in an environment where they had a sense of distance, a greater sense of autonomy, and accountability to others. While this recommendation makes intuitive sense, it is no guarantee. The fact is that there is little research in the family business field that has actually studied the impact of outside work experience, and there are many successors who have had success even though they went straight into the business. Successors who do not get outside work experience must learn to differentiate in the presence of their parents, which in some respects can be much harder.

5

"I Can See Clearly Now"

The origins of a fresh vision for the family business

"I have traveled millions of kilometers for Taittinger and developed a deep philosophy of people, culture ... and who I am ... When you die, people will not judge you by the amount of money you made; they will judge you by the amount of happiness they had with you."

So says Pierre Emmanuel Taittinger, head of the Taittinger Estate and its world-renowned Taittinger Champagne.

The happiness Pierre speaks of is embodied by a glass of champagne.

The Champagne Way, says Pierre, is about "delicacy, elegance, happiness ... and a glass of champagne to get you there more quickly."

With miles of leadership logged, Pierre came to understand that while the Champagne Way is an ideal approach to living, it's not one that's afforded everyone. "I am a very relaxed man," says Pierre, "but I am not relaxed when we spend 5,000 liters to wash a car every two days, and some people do not have water in Africa. When I see that we waste a lot of food, I am not relaxed. When I see that we spend fortunes in ways that are not totally useful, I am not relaxed. I am not relaxed to think that half of the world is not happy. How can you be relaxed? The world is greedy, the world has a lot of corruption; money has taken too much [importance]."

From this perspective, Pierre says of his leadership with Taittinger Champagne, "I am as small as a bubble of champagne." Small and insignificant.

Happiness and humility define the essence of Pierre Taittinger's value system and have shaped his vision. It's not about dying a wealthy man. His vision of greatness is about investing in what his family has called the *human project,* serving others. "Generosity is for me important and we are never generous enough," says Pierre. "It's important for me."

A vision as lofty as the human project demands first recognizing one's humanity, how small one individual is in the big picture. "I'm a simple and modest man and my simple pleasure is to work in the mountains," Taittinger says. "I have 1,700 years of history beneath my feet. I am a servant. In the monastery, one day you are chief, and the next day you become again a very simple monk, and I learned this way of seeing things."

Beneath Pierre's vision is an aquifer of convictions, which give champagne happiness its substance and purpose. He is a third-generation member of the champagne family. Duty and faith are the backbone of his personality (Pierre was educated by the Jesuits), supplemented by an artistic streak he says his mother gave him, and bolstered by the spirit of a warrior, inspired by his Uncle Michel who fought and died in Africa.

Pierre earned his way to the top of the family business, capitalizing on his family's name and history, his personality and ability, and hard work. Pierre's father, Jean, was a soldier, politician, and businessman, who grew Champagne Taittinger into the third-largest estate in the France's Champagne region. Like his father, Pierre served in the military, and then became a salesman in the Champagne region. When a friend suggested the obvious, selling his own family's champagne, Pierre joined the Taittinger sales force. "I served more out of duty than passion." But he quickly found the passion. "To sell the champagne, I had to sell myself, my whole personality. And I discovered that the words to convince the customers came easily." When Pierre became worldwide ambassador for the company, he continued to use his words to inspire and persuade.

Pierre's vision for Taittinger Champagne is as simple and egalitarian as his outlook on life. "I would like to maintain a reasonable price for a bottle of champagne to be able to be part of each life, whether a modest life or a rich life."

Without values, there can be no vision. A successor who searches and lives out his values as well as those of the family business, like Pierre, possesses the internal credibility to cast a vision for the family business. External credibility follows suit as the successor carries out the vision with authenticity.

A Story for the Future: Mission, Vision, and Values

Pierre Taittinger is an apparent contradiction: a simple man who lives the Champagne Way. And he has a vision to bring his champagne values to everyone. But that contradiction speaks to the way in which Pierre has taken family values and created his own vision for the future of Taittinger Champagne. To make your own way requires a healthy understanding of your family, what they have been for you, and how they have helped shape you. It requires a desire to begin to know yourself apart from the dominating influences of your life. Family values run deep in Pierre. Duty, faith, service, and sacrifice. But these values didn't save the company. It took Pierre Taittinger's personal vision to ensure that the family remained the guide of the Champagne Way. In the 1990s, the Taittinger family expanded their business, investing heavily in other luxury products. This eventually led to cash-flow and other financial problems, resulting in the sale of the Taittinger brands in July 2005 to the American-owned Starwood Hotel Group.

The sale was badly received by the champagne-producing community. It feared the new owners would pursue short-term profitability over quality, upsetting the equilibrium of the champagne industry.

Pierre objected to the sale, but wanted to protect his relationship with the family. "We have to respect each member of the family," he says. "I wanted to protect the good atmosphere after and stay in good relationship with all of them. We could not say no."

But he was also fiercely committed to the family business, the tradition, the values, and the personality behind the champagne. When Starwood found itself in the place Taittinger was years earlier—short of cash—Pierre fought to buy it back. On May 31, 2006, members of the Taittinger family resumed ownership of the company.

"We paid a big price," says Pierre, "and that was fine." For Pierre Taittinger it is never about the money; it's always about the champagne and what it can bring to others. It's the Champagne Way. Pierre exhibited a value that was seen across many of the interviews: While money is important, it is values beyond financial success that are critical to one's being.

It took family values plus personal vision to bring Taittinger Champagne back into the fold. Pierre's vision was harnessed to the family legacy, with its history, tradition, and abiding values. His mission was to make the Champagne Way accessible to all, but his vision also found a way forward after the family had cashed it in.

Respect the Past; Do What's Right for the Future

"Respect the past, but always do what's right for the future."

Bill Wrigley's motto speaks for all successors who have successfully managed the process of leveraging family values into a vision for the future of the family business. The visionary leader of a family business has the hindsight to hold onto the foundational values of the organization and the foresight to know what needs to change in order to meet the challenges of the future. A visionary leader generates both meaning and growth.

Earlier in this book, I defined the generative mythology as system-centric. At the center of the family system, the generative leader provides the centripetal force to keep the system in place and the centrifugal force to keep it expanding. This leader is also sociocentric (not egocentric), putting the needs of the family and the business first, and subordinating the leader's own needs.

The concept of the generative leader comes from the archetype of the mythical king in ancient cultures and religions.[1] The king brings order to chaos. The stories we tell as a family reflect the archetypes and beliefs that we have about kingly leadership, and our desire for good kings who use their power and position with compassion to generate the well-being and the productivity of their subjects. "The hands of the king are healing hands; thus shall the king be known," as stated by the legend of Gondor in the third installment of the epic trilogy *Lord of the Rings*.

The anti-type of this archetypical king is the inflated and grandiose leader who deprives his people of selfhood. Applied to family business, this is the leader who establishes a cult of personality that stifles the next generation and deprives them of self-expression. Their inner experience is impoverished and limited.

---

[1] Robert Moore and Douglas Gillette, *King, Warrior, Magician, Lover: Rediscovering the Archetypes of the Mature Masculine* (HarperSanFrancisco, 1990).

The stories told about family business leaders frame the mythology. Often, they create a divine-like image of infallibility and inflate the ego of the leader. Rather than buy into the tyrant king archetype, I would argue that generative successors are more like the kings found in Hebrew scripture, who are described as servants of the Lord, entrusted to lead well, without considering themselves better than the people they led.[2] Mortal leaders subordinate their egos in a much more generative manner. This is due, in part, because they know their place and calling: mortals who serve God and the people.

Moore and Gillette, who wrote *The King Within: Accessing the King in the Male Psyche*, argue that the mortal king is the servant of God rather than the incarnation of God on earth.[3] Too often, however, family business mythologies portray the leader as the incarnation of God on earth rather than God's servant. To distill the characteristics of the generative leader described by Moore and Gillette, the generative leader has three primary characteristics: presence, self-confidence, and objectivity (all characteristics of a differentiated leader). Combined, these qualities enable him to care for and influence others. Presence reveals the self-mastery of these leaders. They are secure and centered, stand firm in chaos, and are not thrown off balance by others. They defend personal boundaries firmly (without hostility), but they also can act aggressively when such a response is necessary. Because they are secure in their identity, they can allow others to be themselves.

Generative leaders are self-confident and don't avoid the truth, especially when it comes in the form of criticism from others. When generative leaders are criticized, they don't lash out emotionally; they take the criticism and seek to understand its relevancy and validity. They see it as an opportunity for continued improvement. Not only are they responsible for their own well-being and the health of the organization, they also take appropriate responsibility when things go bad. Counter to how the mythologies will shape a leader, they are not martyrs, but make personal sacrifices and invest themselves in the business. "When people ask me, 'Why are you working so hard? You own the place,'" says John Tyson, "I tell them, 'That's why I am

---

[2] See, for example, Deuteronomy 17:14–20.

[3] Robert Moore and Douglas Gillette, *The King Within: Accessing the King in the Male Psyche* (Chicago: Exploration Press, 2007).

working so hard. I own the place.' When you choose to run the business, you have to be there."

Generative leaders understand their people; their objectivity makes them effective with those in their care. They are truth tellers but also empathetic, able to evaluate others objectively and with respect and compassion. Their ability to speak the truth and act truthfully helps others become more authentic. They know how to forge unity from disparate viewpoints because they listen to the truth spoken from all sides.

Because generative leaders care for themselves, they can care for others, their families, employees, and community. Edgy business practices, such as risk taking, and the rewards that ensue, are motivated by care and the desire to sustain and grow the organization.

Generative leaders understand that effective leadership inspires people to follow. People grant them the authority to lead because they trust these leaders to have their backs and their best interests in mind. More than that, they protect, celebrate, and inspire the people around them to be and do their best. What they give, these leaders get back tenfold.

The Rudder of Conviction

Values are the rudder that keeps a person, family, and company on course. Vision is setting that course. And our mission is the reason why we take the journey. Values are an extension of what has gone before, building to incorporate the beliefs and passions for the future. The vision is a goal for the future. Put another way, values help bring you to where you are, but they don't get you to where you want to go. The past always informs and shapes the future, but it doesn't provide direction for the future. In a family business, a successor must come to a point of crisis that prompts decisive action to create a new way forward—a fresh vision.

Children don't honor their parents by being like them; they honor them, and perpetuate the family legacy, only by building on what has been given to them. They leverage the legacy with their own talents for bigger and better things for both the family and business. Emulating the past will slowly starve a business of the essential creativity and innovation that a successor's uniqueness brings to it. The way forward is adaptation and progress, not imitation.

According to Massimo Ferragamo, whom we met in Chapter 1, the critical task of the successor is to understand and assess the company culture as well as what he or she can bring to the company. That includes exploring and understanding the company's DNA— that which distinguishes it from all of the other companies operating in that competitive space: what makes the company special. Although human DNA is fixed, a company's is not. Perhaps that's where the metaphor breaks down for a family business. The challenge for the successor is to interpret the culture of the company and add to (or subtract from) it based on his or her unique gifts—and given the context, environment, or needs of the business itself.

The successor must assess which aspects of the tradition are immutable, foundational principles (typically values, like commitment to people and communities) and which need to morph for success in the emerging era (business processes, like technology, products, and sometimes people).

Working with successors for almost 20 years in our Next Generation Leadership Institute and through the interviews with the successors for this book, I have found that successors are more successful when born into a mythology in which the hero—the founder or predecessor—is committed to a purpose larger than any one person's personal feats. The family's values are larger than the individual's success. But successors only find self-fulfillment in the family business when, with a foundation of values, they figure out what they can uniquely contribute to the story. The question is how a successor will sustain the values in a way authentic to his- or herself.

Perhaps the greatest gift that parents pass on to their children are values. Attributes and values are passed down across the generations not only through strands of DNA but also through shared familial and cultural norms. Children absorb values implicitly through *show and tell*—watching the behavior and actions of their parents, including observing what behaviors are rewarded and punished, while absorbing what their parents tell them. They also learn values explicitly through the influence and teaching of community organizations, such as school; church, synagogue, or temple; clubs; and friends.

However, values are knit into our personality and become markers of our identity only when they become beliefs upon which we act by choice. If values are the rudder of conviction that keeps us on course, integrity is the hand on the rudder. Integrity shows itself in the intentional alignment of values—the beliefs and behaviors claimed as important—and one's actions. Short of expression and action, a belief is just an opinion.

Successors are their ideal selves only to the extent that their actions are in alignment with their values; they lose their sense of self when they are out of alignment. When successors default on who they truly are and aspire to be, they forfeit internal credibility. Take the example of a successor who aspired to be a musician. He had proven talent, and pursued music at the collegiate level. When he told his father that his dream was to become a musician, his father's response was, "That's stupid. You are going to study business and come to work for me. You can't make a living as a musician." The sad part of this story is that he decided to give up his passion for music, purely because his father told him it was stupid. In some ways, he gave up a part of himself to his father. He might never have been a successful professional musician—but he never even tried. That same successor is now in his fifties, unhappy being a part of the family business and struggling with depression and low self-esteem. I would argue that if he had taken the opportunity to pursue music, even if he had chosen to go back to the family business at a later date, he would have had better self-esteem and felt that it was more of his choice to be there than his father's.

Working through Personal Values

A person cannot build credibility on borrowed values. A leader must own them. Part of the struggle of growing up in any family is the push and pull of figuring out which family values are one's own, trying them on for size, and experimenting with them. For some, that might mean taking an exploratory trip of other values, by participating in a subculture outside the family. For the successor in a family business, the subculture might be another company, a trip abroad, leadership within the military, or education at a university. A family I worked with had a strong sense of Christian values that permeated both the family and the business. As the family grew and moved beyond its southern, rural roots, the next generation had to take ownership over what those Christian values meant to them, now that they were a larger and more diverse group. The resulting evolution of the family values was built on Christian values of the past, but with new ideas and interpretations that reflected a growing and diverse family.

Many emerging family leaders work out their personal values within the family business, defining values that sometimes wind up in opposition to the parent's. Joe Perrino and his father, Nick Perrino, introduced in Chapter 2, found themselves in a tug-of-war of values: Joe's entrepreneurial energy pulled against his father's approach to protect the business. While Nick feared Home Run Inn's competitors, Joe saw opportunities. Both Joe and Nick *valued* relationships, but only Joe was able to see the *value* of reaching across competitor lines (despite its risk). "Different" did not mean renouncing his father or the company that bore the imprint of his values. Home Run Inn's message today is the same as it was in 1917: Delicious pizza, made with homemade sauces and sausage without a single additive or preservative.

Joe said, "It's how we've done it ever since we opened our original pizzeria on Chicago's South Side. Consider it our family's way of bringing our history home to your family."

People care deeply about the reputation and values of the companies they work for, and none more so than family members in a family business. Tradition and values moor a company through the endless sea of change. Values are sacred. To abandon them is to violate the sacredness of its history and tradition. Change the values, and no longer is there a family business, for values come from human beings.

Too often in family business, the mythology teaches us that the only way that we can add value to the family firm is to be the next CEO of the company. In my nearly 20 years of working with family businesses, I've learned that successful large multigenerational families need leadership of all shapes and sizes. They don't just need a CEO to be successful across generations. They need a strong family council leader. They need leadership on the board, and informally in the family. They leverage the talents of all family members, not just those of their CEO. They tap into the leadership of the daughter, who is the social worker, to lead difficult discussions. They invite the entrepreneurial in-laws to share their talents on the board. The essence is that they honor the talents and passions of all of their family members, and make their participation in the family business a choice.

Family Planning

Nonfamily corporations typically reflect the personality of their CEO. When business booms, the CEO gets the credit. When things go south, the CEO gets the boot, along with a golden parachute. To change the company, the company must change the CEO. A family business, on the other hand, derives its identity from its history, drawing its strength from the unity of the family. It is forged not in the boardroom but around the family dinner table.

"No matter where you go and what you do, you always come back to the family dinner table." This could be the Ferragamo family credo. More than anything else, Massimo remembers the fun. "Having this large family, all working in the company as we grew up, it was fun. And at the dinner table, with eight people, minimum, every night is fun." That also included conflict, which, for a family with strong-minded individuals, was part of the fun. "Six different minds and people can disagree and have different opinions, and discussions in the family can be quite heated sometimes, but when you get up from the table, no one ever left saying, "He wasn't in agreement with me, but I'm going to do it anyway.""

The Ferragamo dinner table was the focal point of family unity, and their center of gravity. Conflict is an indicator of family health when it is incorporated into a common vision that provides direction and purpose for the entire family. Everyone can have their own sense of identity and still pursue the same vision.

Even in their disagreements, the Ferragamos remained a tight family. When any family member had any kind of problem, the rest of the family was there to help. "It's an incredible healing process," says Massimo.

Family unity is forged for a higher purpose than the continuation of the family and its values. It is unified around the opportunities the family business creates for their employees and its mission in the world. According to Alex Hoare, eleventh-generation CEO of private bank C. Hoare & Co., their family values have been translated into a mission of treating others how you would want to be treated—a rarity in the banking world:

> The big oligopolistic banks try to maximize their profits and it shows. They treat their customers and staff like rubbish. We are not trying to maximize our profits, we are trying to create a profitable family business, so we treat our customers and our staff as well as we can. In fact, one of the values which everybody is told when they walk in here is we treat others as we wish to be treated. That is quite unique in British banking. And it really works. When it comes to partners we treat our chargeable trust as an eighth partner. So we give about 10 percent of our net profits. There is a big philanthropic mission going on here.

Family values permeate the culture and act as a compass—a set of guiding principles for both nonfamily and family employees.

Family businesses instill their values into the culture through effective family strategy. Rather than seeing succession planning as a finite process, seeing it as the creation of a family strategy broadens the scope to fully encompass the breadth and depth of the changes that will happen through the succession transitions. A family strategy is much more comprehensive than the traditional succession plan.

Carrying a family business from one generation to the next is not about replacing the parent with the child. It's not that easy. Pierre Taittinger doesn't call it a succession, but a transmission. "I would like to leave at 65-years-old maximum because I think it's safe. It's forced me to organize my future, to organize the transmission." When top management retired, he replaced them with brilliant 30-year-olds, young enough and smart enough to know what they were doing within five years. Pierre also employed two of his children, his son Clovis to be the export manager, and his daughter Vitalie the artistic director. "They are a reflection now" of the Champagne Way.

A family strategy uses the articulation of a clear mission, vision, and strategy and builds them into concrete actions and governance that will unify the family business for generations.

Mission

As I stated earlier, values are nice, but they mean very little if they aren't put into action toward an important goal or purpose. When you start a business, you get to choose your business partners. In a family business, you inherit your business partners. This is why it is critical for each generation to develop a sense of mission. Put another way, each generation of a family business needs to articulate and commit to a reason for being—a mission—that is about more than just money. This is the expression of why we want to be in business together and what can we achieve together, for our families, for our community, for our businesses, that we couldn't achieve alone.

This is the system-centric mission that provides the foundational reasons for the family to sacrifice for each other, their employees, and the business. This mission both taps into the values and the legacy that went before, while looking forward to the impact that a family can have if it works together toward common goals.

Succession planning will not work if there is not also a strategy for family unity. This process must be worked through with the next generation. In a family business, it's not simply a swap-out at the top. It's not merely about replacing the CEO. It's a seismic shift at the base that creates and allows for healthy family conflict.

New leaders in a family business do not heroically swoop in to save a company or take it to new heights. John Burke, Joe Perrino, Bill Wrigley, and Mike Hamra emerged as leaders from the struggle they had with their fathers. That struggle helped shape their identity, strengthen their values, and forge a fresh vision. They are more than just leaders of companies; they are stewards of a legacy. For Pierre Taittinger, the legacy is the Champagne Way, a set of values, and he is only one of many guides who preceded him and in the years to come will follow him.

The trap that some successors fall into is forgetting they are stewards of a legacy; they force change not in keeping with that legacy. An assault on the values of a predecessor is rarely successful. In general, successful emerging leaders create conditions in which the predecessor trusts that the successor has the best interests of both the family and business in mind. The successor must become a *servant* to the family legacy. That includes a respect of its heritage—an appreciation for and understanding of the unique circumstances that shaped the organization to date. Being a servant to the legacy also means operating the business according to family values and defining a vision that reflects the values. Finally, the servant leader has great empathy for the difficulty of change: *What am I asking those who have gone before me to sacrifice?*

Selfishness and dismissiveness are contrary to the very nature of a family business, which is called to serve the greater good rather than the greatness of an individual.

Back to the Future

A grand vision boils down to two questions: Does it fulfill the family business mission? And can we make it happen?

Generative leaders cast an inspiring vision while leaving space for the contributions of other stakeholders, future generations, and often times the contributions of employees and partners. Their values drive strong relationships.

This can be seen in the partnership and relationship between the Taittinger and Kopf families. A partnership created in 1947 and built on a foundation of values by Pierre's Uncle Francois Taittinger and Rudy Kopf of Kobrand Corporation brought "The Champagne Way" to California, launching Taittinger as a brand in the United States.

Building on the alignment in values between Kopf and Taittinger, the families expanded their relationship creating a 50/50 joint venture to build the famous winery Domain Carneros "By Taittinger" in California. Domaine Carneros is now producing and selling more that 700,000 bottles of sparkling wine a year as well as 300,000 bottles of Pinot Noir.

So generative leadership, built on values, can build relationships that can improve on what has been given to it and form a lasting foundation for the next generation.

"When you die," Pierre says, "people will not judge you by the amount of money that you made; they will judge you by the amount of happiness they had with you."

Pierre has a profound understanding of what his family gave him: skills, knowledge, and values. But he didn't stop there; he used his values and leadership to build and expand on the relationships and values that are critical to Taittinger's success.

VISION SEEING BOTH THE WAVES AND THE CURRENTS

Dave Juday, chairman (retired) of Ideal Industries, third generation

Stepping into the leadership of a company founded in 1916 that makes the commitment to create the "Ideal" set of relationships between customers, employees, and communities, a company that has always been profitable, would seem daunting to many. But, at the age of 39, that is what Dave Juday did. While Dave originally had no intention of going into the family business, Ideal Industries is where he ended up. First, though, he did some exploring for several years, doing stints as a Vista volunteer, a schoolteacher, a hearse driver, a bartender, and eventually landing a job in manufacturing. It was working for this manufacturing company that he was able to find his center and a path forward. Dave said this outside work experience was fundamental to helping him establish his values clearly. Gradually, his path led him back to the family company, where he rose through the ranks to become chairman.

In his early years as chairman, building on his values, Dave began to confront some very difficult challenges in his life. In those first years, he "came to grips with a long-standing issue with alcohol, got divorced, quit smoking, and began to try to address some very difficult issues facing Ideal and it's leadership team." Over many years, Dave crafted a vision for Ideal that enabled it to continue to grow while being continuously profitable.

Dave uses a metaphor of the ocean, inspired by the work of Theodore Peredis and Lena Kolocek, to understand the turbulence that often exists in family businesses when thinking about strategy and vision. He stresses the importance of understanding both the waves and the currents:

> The waves are of course what we see, and they can cause major destruction. The fact is that the waves don't move any water, except for up and down in a single column. Their impact [normally] is only within the first few feet of where the water meets the shore. Currents on the other hand are pervasive. They circle the world, they impact climate, the flora and fauna throughout the oceans, and they circle the earth . . . .
>
> If you ask the casual observer of an ocean what it was they noticed, the discussion would quickly turn to waves. And if we call on our metaphor of the ocean for business, I think that very often we are attracted to the waves when we do our strategy planning and look past those currents that are frankly sometimes very difficult to deal with [and often represent the real challenges facing the business]. [An] institution I am aware of, distributed a 400-page document as preparation for a strategic planning meeting and at the same time refused to acknowledge the real current, which was that they did not have capable and competent senior management to be able to execute any plan that was conceived, even with the help of the expensive consultants. The outsiders simply didn't have the insight into the competency of the staff, and the senior management and board were unwilling to take the necessary steps to acquire them.

Dave highlights the importance of not just seeing problems but also looking at the underlying causes that are often more difficult to address. The result is that Dave has led his family to look at the real challenge in moving from the third generation to the fourth generation, creating a sense of stewardship and unity in the family to continue the growth and success of the business. With the help of his daughter Meghan, who leads the family council and a group of dedicated and budding G4 leaders, they have led the family to seek to create an "Ideal" relationship between the family and the business. An indicator of this transformative vision is that the family has actually voted to take a portion of its annual dividends and use it to create a pool of funds to devote to shareholder development. The belief is that in order for the family to be the "Ideal" partner to the business, they must invest their time, money, and energy in making that a reality.

So we can learn from Dave's story that one challenge for a successor is to learn to see both the waves and the currents and create a vision that addresses them both.

Nonstop Learning

Know your weakness and improve

"**I** am damn good at what I do."

That is a statement born from a sense of credibility. Dick DeVos saw his family company, Amway, grow from $500 million in annual sales when he joined the company in 1974 to more than $4 billion in sales when he retired in 2002. The surge started in 1986. DeVos took over a fledgling international department that accounted for less than 10 percent of total revenue. In six years, international revenue exceeded domestic; today it represents 85 percent of revenue.

"I am not very bright," DeVos says, "but I knew enough about all aspects of the business that by the time I took over as president no one could blow a fastball by me. I didn't have all the answers, but I could separate the wheat from the chaff."

DeVos became "damn good" by ascribing to a family value: Life is what you make of it only when you make something of yourself from what you've been given.

Richard DeVos gave his children a head start. They benefited from a fertile heritage rooted in family values. "My father came from a strong Dutch background," says the son. "He had a strong Christian worldview, a strong work ethic, and a solutions-oriented approach to things." Richard conferred his can-do attitude to his children, anticipating that one of them would someday operate the business. He developed a five-year training program in the company that gave his children the opportunity for hands-on training in a variety of departments.

"I had a long-standing record in the warehouse for slowest time loading a truck," Dick DeVos says. "I couldn't keep up with the people in production." Underperforming his co-workers deepened his respect for their talent and how they contributed to Amway's success. DeVos says, "They worked with skill, precision, and intensity on a fast-moving line to make sure that the product was perfect."

"I was born on third base but I learned to hit triples," says DeVos. He capitalized on the opportunities afforded him through training, but he also had an insatiable appetite for learning. He aspired to the perfection that he saw on the assembly line. Like those who did the best with what they had in more restricted roles, Dick understood his capabilities and relentlessly increased their capacity. Dick made the most of small opportunities to hone his leadership skills. He took over the fledgling international business, growing it into the majority piece of Amway. This established credibility with his co-workers, as well as his father and partner.

Richard DeVos started Amway in the family basement, where his son, Dick, played with paperclip chains and paper airplanes and tried to help by moving boxes around. As he grew up, Dick learned to discern his father's intent for the business. "My father never obligated us to join the business, and never overtly stated it, but it was always clear to me that it had to be family driven, and that meant us. I learned to read between the lines." Over time, as he realized that he wanted to join the leadership ranks of Amway, Dick sought opportunities to learn the fundamentals of small business.

Leaders don't get great at what they do by being passive. Instead, they find what they need to learn and figure out how to get it. In the process, they learn how to train their minds to focus on the essential lessons that specific goals call for.

Dick DeVos grasped the "speed of the leader, speed of the team" principle, recognizing that Amway's success demanded a relentless pursuit of his own learning. He followed the principle he learned in high school while working as an understudy to a venture capitalist. He says of the small business, "I could see much more directly the cause-and-effect relationship of every moving part." Learning from the small and extrapolating to a bigger context "is like sailing a small boat to learn how to pilot a much larger boat." An avid sailor, DeVos says, "The mechanics are the same, but the feedback is different. On a small boat, it's instantaneous; do the wrong thing on a sailboat and you flip over. On a big boat, you have so many more variables, more complexity that makes it harder to discern what's needed. The learning is hard. But it's the small boat sailing that gives you the opportunity to learn the big ships."

DeVos wanted to captain the big ship. When he arrived at the top, he probed for what the company was lacking. He says, "While Amway was clearly living a mission driven by the founder's example, that mission hadn't been distilled and documented to establish clear priorities and boundaries. So I established its four pillars of freedom, family, hope, with the goal of a more positive future, and the guiding tenet that reward follows achievement." DeVos saw all of this as a platform from which to make a difference—to support people. "We are compelled to be difference makers, in the family first, and then in others outside our families."

Sustaining Credibility

When your actions and track record support it, "I am good at what I do" is not hubris but an honest self-assessment.

Its counterpart, "I am not that smart," is also an honest assessment. It's the recognition that becoming good at something doesn't mean that you know everything, that humility can create the drive for continual improvement. Both statements reflect a leader's self-awareness, which often forms through the relentless pursuit of self-improvement. While we are born with certain leadership abilities, others can be built through hard work and sweat equity.

This pursuit, along with all the family successor's leadership pursuits I have discussed thus far—stepping out of the shadows of a predecessor, the process of learning through action, developing a mission, vision, and values—are the outgrowth of pursuing differentiation. Differentiation is a process, a long walk in the same direction. It is not a one-time event from which a person moves on to more challenging tasks. It is, rather, an ongoing pursuit of truth, of living from our true selves, bringing forth what is within us, and giving it full expression. Jean Moran speaks of the value of being fully expressive, as her father was: "'I'll tell it like it is,' he would always say, and he did until my mother would tell him to be quiet and stop airing all our dirty laundry in public. 'You don't need to tell everyone everything that's going on in our family,' to which he responded, 'Maybe what's going on with us will help them.' People could relate to him, they connected with him, and I think they loved him."

Strong successors are continually working to differentiate by developing their sense of self, fully expressing it, and always with the thought of helping those in their care, whether it be family, employees, or members of the community. To make a difference is to first be true to yourself—not for the sake of being unique but for the sake of personal fulfillment and the future success of the family business. The ultimate goal is not to be different, but to be true to yourself and your family. As a leader walks the journey of differentiation, he or she earns internal and external credibility. In herself and with those whom she leads, she builds *believability*—that she is ready to lead. Simply, she leads fully aware of what she is and isn't well-equipped for. She leads authentically.

Regardless of past successes, strong leaders don't ignore their weaknesses but always ask, "Where can I improve? What do I need to do to become a better leader?" The challenges of five years ago aren't the same as today; the most credible leaders pursue self-improvement for tomorrow. Continual improvement is a fight to stay in reality, and hence, stay credible. When a leader succumbs to the myth that "I have arrived," he or she risks succumbing to hubris that prevents the family business from moving forward. It also blinds leaders to frailties within the organization, like personnel issues, internal conflicts, or a division that is underperforming.

"How do I continually stay in the reality of the situation?" This is the question that every leader must continually ask to sustain credibility. Leaders are not afraid to test that credibility. In fact, they seek it out. Testing never stops, even when a leader has achieved enormous success, in part because these leaders never stop pushing the limits of their potential.

Just as we need to meet the life cycle challenges of our youth, we also must meet the life cycle challenges that we face in adulthood. This requires continual learning and evolving. In Chapter 2, I discussed the life cycles from birth to early adulthood. But the life cycle and its challenges continue through adulthood. As an individual ages, he or she faces new and different challenges. In mid-life, women (35–45) tend to shift their focus from others (e.g., children) to themselves—what they need to be fulfilled. One can think of it as a move from parent to adult. Men in mid-life (40s and 50s) start to think about realistic outcomes of their professional life, and refocus on the key relationships.[1] All of this demands continual learning. If we rest on our laurels and don't grow and adapt, we will get stuck. Continually pursuing both greater self-knowledge in leadership and technical experience is crucial.

Respectfully Pushing the Limits

Successors who earn external credibility respectfully push the limits of their leadership, perceiving the risk of failing to deliver on their promises. To build credibility is to build small success upon small success. As Ivan Lansberg writes in "The Tests of a Prince":[2]

> Almost all failed successions I've studied involved an ambitious new leader laying out a lofty plan without considering the viability of his or her promises or the risk to the enterprise. Smart successors realize that predictability is essential for earning stakeholder's trust, and initially they search for growth strategies that will deliver results without being too risky. They underpromise but overdeliver, gradually earning the confidence and respect of key constituencies.... Inexperienced successors often work hard at selling the upside of their initiative without conveying the risks they may pose. The moment they start underperforming, they lose stakeholders' confidence.

Earning the confidence of stakeholders is the essence of building external credibility.

When that credibility is earned, the successors can push the succession process forward. It is rare to see a parent just step back and hand over the reins. Most often, the next generation needs to push the process, with a sense of respect and empathy for what they are asking of their parents.

Before successors take over leadership, they have already learned that credibility is built over time. When children learn to differentiate from other members of the family, they build credibility. Jean Moran,

---

[1]D. Levinson, *Seasons of a Man's Life* (New York: Random House, 1978).

[2]Ivan Lansberg, "The Tests of a Prince," *Harvard Business Review* (September 2007), p. 6.

successor of LMI Packaging, saw that she could not compete with her sister's beauty and charm. Instead, she says, "I decided, 'I will get love if I'm responsible and intelligent.' And I spent the rest of my life doing those things, because that is how I got rewarded, when I was responsible and smart."

A leader loses credibility, however, if he is not constantly building it through successes and overcoming failures. Adapting to the new challenges of their lives and career perhaps is one of the reasons leaders often work 70-hour weeks. It's not just because they have a lot of work to do, or that they can't stop. Rather, they relish the challenge of an ever-changing environment that calls for continual improvement and innovation. It's all about the work, not necessarily about career advancement. This is what energizes leaders.

Becoming the leader of a family business involves a dynamic change in the successor's relationship with his or her grandparents, parents, siblings, and sometimes cousins. To move from child (son or daughter) to peer (CEO), from sibling to boss, involves a change in the dynamics of relationships. As we will find in Chapter 9, Lanse Crane faced new challenges in relating to his brother when he moved from being only a brother to also his brother's boss. Children hate to play follow-the-leader when the successor is their sibling. To become the person to whom a brother or sister or a parent is answerable takes a considerable amount of credibility, empathy, and humility. Through this, the successor builds trust.

Defining Success: Future Forward

Richard DeVos and his partner (co-founders) embodied the Amway culture that they wanted to build, and the company rotated toward the magnetic north of their personalities. "The problem with a cult of personality," Dick DeVos says, "is that when the personality dies, that magnetic center is also gone, and a company can wander." It took Richard's son to translate the Amway culture, its ethos and values, into a mission statement. He articulated its ideas and ideals and oriented the company around a vision for its future. Dick parlayed Amway's essential values of freedom, family, and hope into a goal for the future: helping people build better lives.

Success is not arriving at a goal; it is the incremental process of becoming better and better at the things necessary to achieve our goals. Leaders who continue to build the family legacy define success looking forward, not by what they have accomplished. Leaders who pursue continual improvement learn from the past while focusing on future success and what they need to learn to make that success possible. John Burke said that his father's most legendary attribute was his ability to look down the checkerboard a few more moves than anyone else. A leader's long view guides a successor's next move. A successor who continues to build on a founder's legacy must have a comprehensive view of success that harnesses past accomplishments to build a strong future. It is more than beginning with the end in mind. It's believing there is no end. The next accomplishment—and there always is one—is what drives the pursuit of success. This is what keeps the innovator from ever feeling that they have arrived. They are never there; they just get closer. It's not where they want to end up, but the next thing they want to do, that matters the most. The future does not collapse into a terminus but expands into limitless opportunity.

Know Thy Motives

Making a better life by bettering oneself is both universal and deeply personal. Salvatore Ferragamo brought it to America, where his son Massimo continued to drive it forward: "I need to take what I've been given and make it the best that I can make it."

A leader's fire is in the gut. Leaders ignite their passions with that inner fire and continue to stoke it; they don't turn to other people and other ideas to get fired up. These leaders have developed a sense of what they want to accomplish, and are relentless in achieving that goal. As a result, they have enough self-confidence to persevere through the rigorous process of trial and error toward building internal credibility. Self-confidence cannot be borrowed from parents or peers. External validation is powerful but fleeting for those who are constantly craving the applause of the crowd. Self-confidence creates its own applause, as performers no longer play to the crowd but delight instead in their own accomplishment.

Ironically, it is self-confidence that keeps a leader from self-absorption and consequent craving for external validation. Dick DeVos remembers his father as a supremely self-confident leader who was irrepressibly optimistic: "His gift was to encourage others, and he used it to develop all his business relationships." By contrast, DeVos says, "Many first-generation founders of businesses can be extraordinarily self-absorbed so that they don't have the energy to encourage others. They need to be right, to compete, and to succeed so that they can be on top to be seen and applauded by others. The instincts that drive success in business, if misapplied, can drive family members away."

DeVos makes an important distinction. It's not the desire for success, but the desire misapplied, that frays the family ties that bind a business together. Motivation is everything. Internal motivation to continually improve wards off the complacency that comes when one is externally motivated.

Leaders who are externally motivated rise only to the level of others' expectations, which are either too high or too low and rarely as realistic as the leader's own. Many leaders provide a compelling rationale for this external motivation. Jean Moran's father handed her the company legacy, and she made a vow: "There was no way I was going to let this business fail." She didn't want to let her father down. As noble as this promise sounds, it betrays a fear of disappointing a person, and it is not nearly as powerful a motivator as self-approval. Jean Moran kept learning about the company, but she also kept working on herself, and understanding her motivations, so that later in her career she realized, "I was trying to do what I thought would get everyone to love me. As long as I do the best that I can, that is all I need to do." Through leadership coaching, reflective retreats, and being open to the input of others, Jean was able to better define success for herself.

Massimo Ferragamo brings an even deeper insight about the internal release from trying to please someone else. "When I know I have done the best I can, there is almost an internal forgiveness. I don't have to be my parent." This realization helps the successor become the owner in his or her own right. If a successor owns his or her goals and objectives, and takes the time to develop a unique vision, he or she will own that vision. The motivation to achieve that vision is extremely high. Like Moran, leaders don't want the family business to fail on their watch. Conversely, if a successor adopts a hand-me-down mission (and vision of his or her parents), he or she won't own the mission in the same way. Nor will he or she be motivated to continually improve. The reasoning goes, "If it is not my mission, then I won't own it. And I won't be passionate about or accountable for achieving the mission."

A person's sense of what he wants to accomplish helps him understand what it takes to get there, what he is able to do, and the help he needs to do what he can't. This is why the most credible leaders build strong teams around themselves. They understand that being the best they can be is not limiting when they have the self-confidence to make themselves better by making people around them better. That is the opposite of self-absorption.

The Necessity of Continual Development

Stepping out of the founder's shadow is to step into the sunshine. Many successors prefer to remain in the shadows, though, because the light exposes who they are. Yet that is the necessary starting point for the work of continual self-development—reality.

As I've already argued, the mythology that surrounds a legendary founder helps those who follow find their footing. It provides a context for organizational values. The trouble is that it is hard for successors to step out of the myth and establish their identities in the reality of their abilities and limitations. Just as a myth conceals a legendary founder's mortality, weaknesses, and failures, successors can also perpetuate a myth, often unintentionally, to conceal their own vulnerability. *What if I'm not really a strong enough leader to make this business a success?*

It is easier to escape into a myth of invulnerability than it is to engage in the hard and honest work of continual development. Relentless pursuit of self-improvement punctures the myth that an initial success is an ultimate success. It wards off the mindset, "I have arrived." It embraces the inherent vulnerability present in leading and creating a dynamic vision. A little success goes a long way only when leaders do not use it as an excuse to rest on their laurels and instead use it as impetus for further success.

Vulnerability, along with true humility, is the quality of character that most contributes to the work of continual improvement. The leader who is vulnerable and humble refuses to hide in the shadow of the predecessor's mythology and resists creating his own myth. He or she welcomes failure because it reveals what must be mended in order to build future success.

Dick DeVos did two things crucial to his continual development. First, as I have already noted, he demythologized his iconic father by stripping away the cult of personality that surrounded Richard DeVos. His son acknowledged the mortal behind the myth, and the mortality that would eventually extinguish the personality. Dick DeVos says, "A personality is inherently time-limiting, because personalities die." In addition, a huge personality can only carry ideas and values so far if systems are not in place to reinforce them and continue them into subsequent generations. A personality inspires, but values are the substance of the company that people care deeply about. Dick DeVos established a framework for those values that ensured that the American way would continue to provide economic opportunity and ownership to thousands.

Second, Dick DeVos refused to ride on his success. He became exceptional at his job, in part because he understood that the hard work of continual learning would compensate for not being the smartest man in the world. But he was smart enough to know that intelligence is not a fixed quantity. People can raise their IQ by challenging their minds, especially when they apply their minds to goals they want to achieve. And Dick DeVos did just that: "I was a builder-creator. I built and continued to create the business with new ideas, new approaches, that took it to a higher level of performance in multiple dimensions."

Leaders who learn from their past to build a vision of the future tend to ground themselves in reality. They seem to be able to accept feedback that reveals their gaps and strips away illusions. Strong leaders do not indulge themselves with illusions. They base their reasoning on actual facts, of which they see the essence. They do not commit the sin of believing in their own mythology, or, as Napoleon Bonaparte once described, of "making pictures" of the world as one wishes it to be, rather than as it is. The generative leader builds a system for getting realistic and practical feedback on their performance on a regular basis. They use criticism as motivation and encourage honesty and forthrightness. This feedback is the fuel for continual learning.

Disciple of the Disciplines

The handmaiden to self-development is self-control. Leaders who are servants to a calling and legacy have learned to master themselves. Their constraint and self-discipline give them the self-assurance they need to lead the organization through its highs and lows. In crisis, people do not look for the most charismatic and eloquent leader; they look for the person who knows what to do and does it decisively. This is the leader who has already tested him- or herself, made critical decisions, and taken responsibility for his or her life and the lives of employees.

Successors who perceive themselves as victims, even subtly, are debilitated by persistently looking outward. They look for someone to blame, while those who take responsibility look relentlessly within. They change themselves. When Mike Hamra came to the crossroads to stay with or leave Hamra Enterprises, he was clear with his father: "Unless we work something out, I'm leaving because this is not working for me." In other words, "If this doesn't change, I need to go." As Mike remembers it, his initial approach smacked of blame and indignation bordering on self-pity. He said, "Headquarters was my father's domain and I was kept out … you promised a succession plan and never followed through … I felt embarrassed … I had a great career and gave it up for you … ."

However, when Mike shifted his orientation from what he demanded to what his father needed, the onus of responsibility shifted from his father to him: "I can change if my dad won't." He began to think of ways to keep his father involved with the business. Mike followed Victor Frankl's dictum, "When we are no longer able to change a situation, we are challenged to change ourselves." Mike took ownership of himself, his emotions, and the company in a way that included his father.

Self-confidence is not the absence of fear or doubt; it is, rather, the ability to recognize these emotions and move forward in spite of them. Emotions are a natural and normal response to external stimuli. The differentiated leader is one who can sit with the emotion and provide a measured and thoughtful response. Emotional health is not the ability to release emotion, to "let it all out." Rather, it is the ability to recognize our emotions and to develop the skill to manage them, especially when the situation calls for a measured response. Family myths tend to distort reality. Uncontrolled emotions cause the same kind of distortions, and lend themselves to creative storytelling. Children are known to tell "whoppers" when punishment is imminent; fear drives the telling of the tall tale. Adults have the same propensity to create stories that are emotionally driven, especially when they feel that they have been slighted or misunderstood. The more insecure and fearful of vulnerability a successor is, the more emotions escalate and stories follow.

I have discovered that the best way of dealing with insecurities is to be honest about one's vulnerability with people that you trust and in an environment that is safe and free from blaming: Invite people you trust into your internal dialogue, and listen to their feedback. It reveals reality while pulling one back to the discipline of self-improvement. Having a support system (coaching, mentors, friends) is essential to managing your own vulnerabilities. When leaders seek out honest feedback, they verify their intuition with the facts. They are more alert, more intellectually active, and less willing to be satisfied with superficial answers. These are emotionally healthy leaders because they lead with an acknowledgment of their feelings, balanced with the objectivity of their mind. They are mentally tough.

Staying Power

The finest steel seeks out the hottest furnace. And it stays in the fire. Leaders who have undergone rigorous testing are able to make hard decisions and take on bigger challenges for the good of the business they lead. The discipline of relentless self-improvement is perhaps most focused on the task of not giving in. Leaders worth their mettle develop a relentless focus on their vision and goals.

Ocean vessels have a dynamic positioning system that automatically maintains their position through propellers and thrusters. The most interesting feature of this system is that it allows a ship to remain stationary without the use of mooring or an anchor while it conducts operations at sea. That which moves the ship also keeps it still. Relentless self-improvement has a forward trajectory as a leader pursues his or her vision and achieves his or her goals, but it's precisely that momentum that gives leaders the resolve to maintain their heading and their position, after they have set a determined course. In psychological terms, this is having an internal locus of control, and is defined as the extent to which individuals believe that they can control the events affecting them. Its opposite is a lack of focus, when a leader allows an external array of forces to control him. This leader scrambles, responding to whatever it is that exerts the most influence over him at the moment. Leaders who continually change their direction and focus tend to have a victim's mentality: They are victims of circumstance. They don't have any control, so they don't act in a way that exhibits control. The internal locus of control is their inner orientation of core values and purpose. American poet TS Eliot describes it this way: "The still point of the turning world … there the dance is."[3] Such leaders hold their position and are patient, not just quiet but still within, so that they can listen and discern the forces of wind and wave.

Of his own ability to make current decisions based on his prescient future projections, Dick DeVos says, "Others could not see the dangers ahead that I saw, and thus could not understand the radical changes and the difficult decisions required to change course and to stay there." A leader's self-discipline of continual self-development creates the inner confidence to be internally stable and not waffle when others doubt his or her choices to grow the company and extend the family legacy.

Dick DeVos took Amway to a higher level of performance with new ideas and fresh approaches, but he had to forge a steely resolve, a harder edge, than his father had. The business was struggling: Profitability was down, and DeVos had to eliminate 1,400 jobs in a restructuring of the company. It was the first time in its history that Amway had undergone a mass layoff. At the same time, he also forced the two founding fathers to either buy or sell a cherished asset that they both loved, an island hotel operation that was not core to the business.

It is the commitment to leadership that combines an insatiable desire to learn, as well as a tenacity to refine one's abilities to achieve one's objectives. It is the coming together of these elements that makes successors run farther than their predecessors. It's not any one gift, capability, or talent. It's a combination of attributes, all focused on the larger purpose of writing the next chapter of the family legacy.

---

[3]T. S. Elliot, Burnt Norton, *Four Quarters* (1935), section II.

CHAPTER 7

Feed the Family

Caring for relationships, caring for the business

Jean Moran earned the title *the enforcer* honestly when she terminated the employment of her younger brother.

The second child in the family, Virginia (Jean) succeeded her father as CEO of LMI Packaging Solutions, an innovator of flexible lidding solutions for food packaging that has partnered with food industry leaders like Coca-Cola, Kraft, and Procter & Gamble.

Early in her rise to leadership, Jean faced family challenges that she calls "exhausting." Smart, responsible, and resourceful—Jean's leadership qualities were apparent in her teen years, and soon she had the ear of her father. He began to confide in her.

"The relationship he could have had with a first born son, or my younger brother," Jean says, "he had with me." Jean spent her free time with him at his work, while her siblings did things that were more normal for their ages. Jean earned her father's respect as a young adult, solving complex problems at work that her father refused to solve for her: "You're a smart girl. You'll figure it out." And she would.

But some conundrums aren't easy to solve, especially when family is involved. "I think that it was tough for my younger brother." Jean says, "because I was the 'son' that took over the business." When the department he managed failed to perform, Jean fired her brother. Although it was ultimately the right decision, she says, "I went about it the wrong way, and blindsided him. He was shocked. I could enforce, but I couldn't communicate. I avoided constructive conflict like the plague and had no clue what 'supporting people to accountability with clear communication' meant."

The *family* in family business creates a unique complexity to leadership that is generally not present in publicly traded companies. Jean had to tend to the business while also looking after the best interests of the family. Early on in her leadership, Jean struggled to find a balance.

Jean's mistakes, however, were her greatest lessons. When another family challenge cropped up, much like one she had watched her father fail at years earlier, this time she amended the approach. After years of working with her brother-in-law, Tony, Jean realized that he had outgrown his position at LMI Packaging Solutions. He needed to run his own company. To avoid further family trauma, Jean hired consultants to help the family resolve its issues. They met with Jean and Tony and the other involved family members for an entire weekend to resolve the conflict. The mediation led to Jean retaining leadership of the company, but this time the process was thorough. "Tony now runs his own business," Jean says, "and our conversations are better. We both learned from the experience and have greater respect for each other's talents."

Jean likens communication in a family business to a multicolored beach ball. "Everyone lives on a different color of it," she says. "No one can see the whole beach ball. [My] responsibility is to see the whole ball. You've got to talk to everyone on every single color, because everyone has their perspective."

Jean leads LMI Packaging Solutions with strength as well as humility. She terminated employees who needed to be fired while turning an ear to employees and family members—even when the critique was harsh. Through it all, the business has thrived and the family members spend weekends together in northern Wisconsin's Door County.

It is a rare leader in a family business who can both create a stronger business and nurture family relationships. But the most successful successors understand that a unified family is the foundation for a family business that can last for generations. The family is the business's greatest asset, but most often the successor's biggest challenge. Managing the multiplicity of family personalities, ideas, and motives is complicated. When a successor rises to leadership, she can't shut out the family and just run the business like a business. She has to understand the importance of the family to the business and implement strategies to unify the family. These strategies can be as simple as having regular family meetings or as complex as creating a family council and constitution to govern the work of the family.

Many successors have a credibility problem with other family members. And it is job one to pay attention to building family credibility. Ignoring the family's input leads to hurt feelings and, ultimately, disengagement and disunity. Family unity is as important as what shows up on the balance sheet. Unified families tend to be able to focus on the larger purpose of the family business: create jobs, invest more in their employees, commit to customers, and give back to the community. When family shareholders understand both the financial and nonfinancial impact of the company, they can support the long-term approach that isn't just focused on short-term profits.

The common mentality among thought leaders in the field of family business has been to protect the golden goose (the business) at all costs. But the golden goose isn't the business; it's the family. If a family leader protects the business at all costs, she often sacrifices the family relationships—and the legacy that can sustain it across generations.

The successor's primary job is to grow the family assets while preserving and enhancing its legacy. Generative successors should understand that while they must run a great business, they can't forsake the family relationships. Simply, the more emotionally connected a family is to the business and its values and the more connected its members are to each other, the more support successors will have as they lead the family business into the next era.

Dare to Be Different

Building credibility and trust with family members is a process that begins well before the succession of the founder, as the successor demonstrates consistency in actions and words. Successors who have problems with this early in life might have to work hard to rebuild that trust. Jean Moran's pathway to credibility at LMI Packaging Solutions was not easy. Jean was handpicked by her father, Chester Sykes, to lead the business he had founded in 1967, Label Makers, Inc. Nevertheless, she had to establish her credibility with siblings who had varying levels of interest in and commitment to the company. Jean didn't fully comprehend it at the time, but every time she set herself apart from her siblings, she deepened her sense of who she was.

Every time Jean went to work with her father, she differentiated herself from her siblings and potential to be the successor.

Jean had no idea that her reward for acting responsibly would one day be leadership of the family business, and that the family was already testing her physical, emotional, and intellectual capacity. The tests continued until she faced the ultimate test of her credibility: Do the tough things that were needed for the longevity of the business and still keep the welfare of the family front and center.

Throughout the book, I've argued that it's the differentiated leader who is most likely to lead the family business successfully. In this instance, an undifferentiated successor might have said, "I can't fire my brother. It will cause too much turmoil in the family." But the *differentiated* successor discerns when to sacrifice for the sake of the larger objectives of the family enterprise. The business and family legacy won't survive if the hard family decisions aren't made. Too often, successors resist holding siblings accountable, fearing family friction. Appearances may reflect unity, but the unity is a myth, built on the premise of avoidance: *We won't talk about anything that puts us into conflict. We won't talk about difficult things.* The undifferentiated leader tends to respond instinctively to familial emotional outbursts. He or she may seek to placate family members rather than stand in the presence of the conflicted family emotion and do what's right for the family *and* the business with empathy. In addition, she becomes a participant in the family drama, rather than leading the process of attending to the underlying emotions of the family. For example, when a family shareholder directs emotionally charged criticism at the CEO, the undifferentiated response will be to either lash back or ignore it. The differentiated response is thoughtful engagement that seeks to understand the perceptions behind the emotion as well as address the relationship. "Let's have a conversation about this, because I would like to understand this. If there is something important for me to know, I need to learn it."

This differentiated response takes humility, character, and a strong sense of self, what I've called "internal credibility." Without that, a leader reacts out of fear and insecurity. She fears she won't be liked. She fears critique. She fears she will make the wrong decision. She fears the family crisis will become all-consuming and distract from the daily operations. Successful leadership in a family business depends on an emotionally neutral approach to family crises. That is difficult to do.

Jean Moran did not shrink from confrontation. This demanded managing her emotions so she could manage the ensuing familial maelstrom of emotions. Jean presented her siblings, who had stock in the company but were inactive in the business, with a plan to buy them out. Rather than acquiesce, they unleashed their true feelings: "This business would be doing so much better if our husbands were running it."

"It was good … all this stuff they had never told me," Jean says, "but all this ugliness was on the table, and I walked into the adjacent room and cried like I had never cried before." Through tears came revelation. "I thought I was doing it all for my family. I wasn't doing it for them. I was doing it for my need to be loved." She had created her own mythology that she could make her siblings love her through her work. Then it hit her. She didn't need to earn her family's love. She already had it. The epiphany led to freedom. No longer did she lead to be loved; she did what was best for the organization as well as the family. "Everything turned around that day: my life, the business, my relationship with the family."

Heart and Soul

"If you love them you stay in the game. They're family. You never walk away." The seminal advice Jean received from her mother underscores the reason family businesses achieve success over the long term.

Family businesses are stereotyped as old-fashioned, rife with conflict, lacking scale, and burdened by backward thinking. The prevailing bias is that they can only do well when they behave like public companies. However, the opposite is true. Family businesses comprise approximately 75 percent of all American businesses and account for over half of American jobs, and produce 78 percent of all new jobs.[1] They make up 35 to 40 percent of the Fortune 500 and S&P 500. Family businesses have a myriad of areas where they outperform public companies, including higher financial performance, lower risk profiles, longer survival rates, and higher human and capital investments.[2]

---

[1]J. Astrachan and M. C. Shankar, "Family Businesses Contribution to the US Economy: A Closer Look," *Family Business Review* 16 (3) (2003): 211–219.

[2]D. Miller and I. LeBreton-Miller, *Managing for the Long Run* (Boston: Harvard Business School Press, 2005).

The same holds true in Europe. Research by Herman Simon in his book *Hidden Champions* showed that of 500 mid-sized European firms that dominated their markets, 75 percent were family-owned businesses. These businesses have revenues below $4 billion and a low level of public awareness, but they were number one, two, or three in the world in their market, or they were number one on their continent in market share.

Why is this?

They are close to their customers so there are high switching costs (the costs of switching to a competing company); they tend to compete on quality, total cost of ownership of the product, high performance, and consultation with the customer; they earn their leadership in the market through performance rather than pricing.[3] As a result, family businesses have higher margins of ROE, ROS, & ROA.[4]

Miller and Lebreton-Miller in their book *Managing for the Long Run* cite that the primary reason family businesses are successful is they have continuity as a goal and are willing to sacrifice for it.[5] Because they are invested in a mission, they relentlessly pursue their core capabilities, exercise stewardship, and foster lengthy executive tenure. They have a connective tissue that can't easily be severed. Intently focused on building community, family businesses have a tribal mentality, where loyalty, duty, and obligation (both to the family and to the mission of the family business) connects the enterprise to a purpose greater than profit. The tribal mindset does not preclude an outward focus on being good neighbors and partners. Family businesses are highly respected in their communities. This is true of "mom and pop" businesses and of behemoths like Nordstroms and Ford, where the family ties, albeit diffused, still carry influence. Families who work together toward a legacy tend to stay together—and their businesses tend to thrive. The glue to all of this is the family, which the generative successors must handle carefully. Successful successors cultivate this.

For most family business shareholders I meet, dividends are a piece of what they expect out of the business. However, they are

[3]H. Simon, *Hidden Champions: Lessons from 500 of the Worlds' Best Unknown Companies* (1996).

[4]D. Miller and I. LeBreton-Miller, *Managing for the Long Run* (Boston: Harvard Business School Press, 2005) p.14

[5]D. Miller and I. LeBreton-Miller, *Managing for the Long Run* (Boston: Harvard Business School Press, 2005) p.32

more connected to the legacy and power of what the family does for the community, its employees, and its customers. With legacy as the focus, family members tend to be more committed to the success of the business and less concerned about dividends.

Family businesses most often take the long view. They are patient, willing to invest for the long term, and remain steadfast during economic downturns.[6] They have a broader perspective, have a more comprehensive approach to prosperity, and honor values beyond earning money. They also may take a more personal approach to business based on trust.

"We've known since the 1930s," says Bella Hoare, a partner and one of the eleventh-generation owner-managers at C. Hoare & Co. bank, "that we're the last deposit-taking banks from the era, standing as a family business; we've had 80 years of being unique." Bella's cousin, Alexander Hoare, adds, "And we are the most profitable bank in the country." When most European banks were troubled, they made a fortune, with a return on equity of about 10 percent. The partners of C. Hoare understand a basic principle that is the lodestar for successful family businesses: Businesses are the apparatus for economic transactions, but they don't drive the wealth; people do.

One of the bank's more charming rituals occurs every summer, when Alexander Hoare lays out the bank's entire balance sheet on one sheet of paper and sends it out, with a personal note, to all the bank's customers. Such service reflects the bank's corporate values, "which are derived from our personal values," says Alex, "and are unique in this industry. Instead of trying to maximize our profits, we treat customers as we wish to be treated; we have seven partners and treat our charitable trust as an eighth partner, so we can give away 10 percent of our net profits."

The values carry through in unique ways. Bank staff members found a nanny for a customer within 24 hours; quickly wired cash to a customer's daughter stranded in remote South America; and helped deliver a calf. Because they know each customer personally (or, at least, are familiar with the customer's finances), the Hoare cousins personally approve (or turn down) every major loan to a client, delivering their decision within hours of a request. While C. Hoare & Co. provides the same retail clearing services as the larger clearing banks, it competes on dimensions where it has the clear advantage: relationships, flexibility, care, independence, and speed of service.

---

[6]D. Miller and I. LeBreton-Miller, *Managing for the Long Run* (Boston: Harvard Business School Press, 2005) p.26.

Successful family businesses recognize that the family—not the business—is the golden goose. Many organizations flip this model, but not C. Hoare & Co. It has a large and prolific family golden goose: "Because we are in the eleventh generation, we have over two hundred living cousins in our database. Our normal hiring procedure is to find the best cousin around at the time." Seven Hoare cousins sit on the partners' board of the bank, each "enjoying" unlimited personal liability, which means they are personally on the hook for every asset the bank holds, right down to their cufflinks. Family partners share a mutual and sacrificial commitment that locks them into the family's fortune (or fate). Each partner is "all in," entirely invested in the family business and enjoying its success.

Family Assets

Author and business management consultant Peter Drucker famously compared profit to oxygen: "If you don't have enough of it, your out of the game. But if you think your life is about breathing, you are really missing something." Family is what money can't buy in the family business; family gives the business a reason to live, and a *joie de vivre*. When your family name and legacy is at stake, then there is a greater sense of responsibility for its future.

Mike McKee, CEO of McKee Foods, maker of Little Debbie's snack cakes, calls on the moral capital of his family business to sustain the family legacy: "When a family's values, virtues, norms, practices and identities mesh well with evolved psychological mechanisms." To put it more simply, Mike says, "A strong moral capital is when everyone in the business sings from the same songbook. They know the values, believe in them, and live by them. As a result, cooperation trumps selfishness, employees are more engaged, change is met with speed and agility, talent is retained, and the business develops a strong offensive against intruders."

Family businesses can be nimble and demonstrate strength in the face of market downturns (contrary to the popular misconception that they are weakened by nepotism and tolerate perpetuate incompetence). They have the advantage of being able to more quickly seize opportunity, and reinvent themselves with each new generation. But this is largely predicated on the unity of the family.

Research by Pieper and Astrachan[7] has shown that, for long-standing family businesses like Taittinger Champagne and C. Hoare & Co., there are four main aspects to the sense of cohesion of the family that keep them together across generations. The companies in their study survived for over 200 years and continued to thrive (often in industries different than the original). They do so by remaining simultaneously attentive to both the financial as well as the emotional well-being of the business *and* family members.

Specifically, there are four driving forces behind their success: business financial (the financial success of the business); family financial (the use of family financial resources to help each other); business emotional (the sense of pride, identity, and status that family members derive from being associated with the business); and family emotional (the basic sense of connection members have to each other).

While Pieper and Astrachan found that all four of these components are prevalent among family businesses that survive 200+ years, the most interesting of their findings is that financial variables alone are insufficient for the sustenance of a family business across multiple generations. In order to persist from generation to generation, family members must be connected to each other and to a sense of pride in their economic enterprise. They must embrace what it means for the stakeholders. Financial markers, while basic, alone cannot provide longevity. The intangibles that do not appear on a balance sheet—pride, loyalty, and sacrifice—often keep the family business in the black. Over the generations, these families have learned to protect the golden goose. If the family is the economic engine of its business, trust is the family's currency.

Successors who protect the business at all costs (and sacrifice family relationships in the process) lose sight of the next generation. They operate out of a fear of the family. Certainly, the business is important, but what's going to prevail—the family or the business? Protecting the business at all costs, a successor risks losing the family, and then what does a successor really have? Successful generational

---

[7]T. Pieper and J. Astrachan, *Mechanisms to Assure Family Cohesion: Guidelines for Family Business Leaders and Their Families* (Cox Family Enterprise Center, 2008).

family businesses have learned that protecting the business at all costs is a Pyrrhic victory that detracts from the family legacy.

I'm obviously not saying that successors shouldn't invest in the business. Without reinvesting in the company, the company (and the legacy) dies. But a hyper-focus on investment without consideration of the family members whose assets are being invested can lead to diminishing return. Sam Schwab , a CEO of a substantial apparel and retail firm, recently spoke with me about the complexity of not sacrificing the family for business gains. He says of a new business venture: "I could have asserted that I should have a much more sizable ownership stake based on my role and contribution. I spearheaded the growth and new businesses we entered. But I looked down the line and thought, 'What would the impact be on my relationship with my siblings and cousins 20 years from now? What model would I be setting for the relationship between my own children when they grew?' It wasn't worth the additional money to jeopardize those relationships moving forward. I was confident and preferred that collectively we could grow and succeed together."

Not all family business CEOs think like Sam Schwab. I am aware of a $500 million business that over the last 50 years has reinvested all its profits into the business. Share values have gone up significantly, but members have no liquidity; they are paper rich and cash poor. One family member took a second job at an accounting firm over Christmas so that they could afford to buy gifts for her children. I can only imagine the resentment that built and the impact that would have on their relationships with family members working for the business.

As startling as this scenario sounds, this mentality is prevalent among family businesses that continue to perpetuate a particular aspect of the myth of the founder: protect the business and increase its financial capital at all costs, even at the expense of the family's well-being. They are not able to separate themselves from the business and its success. Bill Wrigley Sr. could never stop working because The Wrigley Company was his life; the business consumed him, and he carried its burden, up to 18 briefcases full of its weight, wherever he went. When it comes to the businesses they create, many family business leaders have a singular mindset: "It's me against the world, and my business success has to prove my worth against all competitors." Such a competitive mindset reflects the American ethos of the rugged individualist. It is undoubtedly helpful in the founding of a business. But for a business to succeed through generations, this mindset must evolve into a more collaborative approach that values family morale and buy-in as much as financials.

The successor needs to make sure that the return on investment is both financial *and* emotional. The greater the emotional return, the lower the pressure on the financial return and the more the family can take the long-term view. The challenge for the successor is to hang on to the values passed on through the myth while stepping out of the shadow of the founder. It is then that the successor will be most authentic to him- or herself and to those whom he or she leads.

How Competition Can Cripple

When the competitive spirit becomes too much a part of the family culture, it can cripple a business. The founder of one family business I studied had his two sons compete to run and own the business (five years each) to show who was the better candidate. To this day, they have not been able to completely repair the damage. Apart from the antagonism it creates, this kind of "may the best man win" mentality is overly simplistic. It fails to factor in a myriad of important variables, such as luck and timing. It fails to realize that the long-term success of the family enterprise will require these brothers to work together and compromise.

Most family business cultures are not this blatantly competitive, but leaders must be vigilant against the development of an "us versus them" mentality, especially among successors and cousins who haven't spent a lifetime collaborating and negotiating. This mentality can show up in a variety of different ways. For instance, a family branch can compete against another family branch; or family members working within the family business can compete with family members working outside the family business. Competition becomes especially gnarly when family members become hyper-focused on what is good for the individual—and not what's good for the whole. A healthy family can balance these competing priorities.

Unhealthy competitiveness (when members focus on "I" versus "we") tends to surface when a business values financial success above all else, and money becomes the only measure of success. A tell-tale sign of poor health in a family business is when the talk excessively revolves around money and its distribution. When relationships are strained or nonexistent, financial capital fills the vacuum and relationships disintegrate. Family members in the business may feel that shareholders outside the business only want money and more of it. Shareholders may perceive that the family members operating the business are living on easy street, enjoying the good life. Preoccupation with money and perceptions surrounding it creates an antagonistic environment. When this happens, the successor has significant work to do to build a sense of connection and trust among family members.

Sharing leadership with siblings, cousins, and other distant relatives demands creating commonality. Ivan Lansberg describes the process:

> To neutralize challenges to their authority, effective successors develop a vision for the enterprise and find ways to connect it to stakeholders' wants and needs. They, in effect, become the weavers of a shared dream that represents the synthesis of stakeholders' aspirations. They also manage to imbue enough of their own identity into the dream to claim it as their own.[8]

Although the myth of the founder helps establish this shared dream, it most often is identified, developed, and passed on through conversation. One successor who stepped into a family business rife with strife, between the family members working for the business and those who did not, sat down with each shareholder individually and had a conversation about the problem. He said, "The past is the past. We can't change it. But what can we do moving forward?" In attempting to find out what was important to each family shareholder, he built a shared vision for the family moving forward. This successor knew that successfully running the day-to-day operations of the business was not enough. To build a foundation for future generations, he needed to build family unity.

From the Founder to the Family

The true heroes of family businesses are those who diffuse their success among the family base and create businesses with momentum, which change and adapt and have impact on their employees as well as their communities.

---

[8]Ivan Lansberg, "The Tests of a Prince," *Harvard Business Review* (September 2007).

The challenge for successors is to shift the focus and the base of the business from the founder to the family. For some successors, the groundwork for this model is already established. Massimo Ferragamo's mother translated her iconic husband's singular vision and talent to her children in such a way that all of them felt that they were carrying his work and his spirit forward. Massimo says, "She was able to establish a harmony between the business [my father built] and all of us that has become the foundation of our family." As his mother led them, so Massimo, the youngest of the Ferragamo siblings, seeks to lead, "not by authority but by example."

Working with the family is the ongoing challenge for the leader of any family business. It's often messy, but the family business can thrive when the family leader cares for the true golden goose, the family. He or she must govern the family as intentionally as running the business itself. Lansberg writes, "The greatest challenge any newly anointed CEO faces is turning stakeholders into followers ... He or she must cope with family members, especially siblings and cousins whose support may be vital to control the enterprise ... "[9] The process of feeding the family is, in essence, caring for the relationship: "I need to build a relationship with you so that I can understand what is important to you and build a shared vision for the family moving forward." Leaders are "weavers of a shared dream" so that a family can be unified about where they are going and what they are doing with their assets. When they have this shared dream, they can do amazing things.

The fear of many successors is that they will get sucked into the black hole of family needs, away from the day-to-day business. If a family business doesn't have strong governance and the right advisors, this can happen. But the most successful successors make sure that family practices, governance, and advisors are in place to pay attention to the needs of the family. When the family is attended to, it will operate so well as a unit that the successor can be totally focused on what the business needs.

Leaders need help. If a leader tries to run the business and govern the family, he or she will exhaust him- or herself and do both poorly. A successor who has differentiated him- or herself from the founder knows he or she doesn't need to lead everything, especially not the family. He or she just has to believe that the family

---

[9]Ibid.

is important enough to pay attention to it, devote resources to it, and raise up other leaders to attend to it. A differentiated leader prioritizes care of the family and facilitates the process of family care.

When Jean Moran fired her brother and was on the verge of a confrontation with her brother-in-law for leadership of LMI Packaging Solutions, she wisely suggested hiring outside consultants to clarify the issues and suggest a solution. Doing so led to an outcome that allowed everyone to win. "We got it right this time," Jean said.

Family governance is not triage, a reaction to family crisis. Rather, leaders provide primary care for the family and ensure its health by putting practices into place that minimize crisis and create opportunities for the family and the business. It's a synergy, with the family working so well that a leader can focus on what the business needs. Dave Juday of Ideal Industries, along with his daughter Meghan, the family council chair and a group of dedicated family leaders, convinced family members to take a share of the dividends and put them in a fund for shareholder development. A portion of every dividend declared goes into this fund, which family members can use for continuing education to help become better stewards of the family business legacy. For example, if a family member aspires to a role of leadership in the family or on the board, he or she will create an Individual Development plan, from which specific action steps will be identified. Once the plan is approved by the group, activities in pursuit of this plan will be funded. It's not a giveaway, and because the dividends fund it, it does not take away from the company. Perhaps the strongest family value is valuing the family, because doing so pays huge dividends for the company.

Family practice boils down to good communication. As Jean Moran simply puts it, "You stay put and you keep talking." When the talking gets difficult, when ideas and personalities conflict, it's time bring in coaches so that all the family, as Mike McKee says, "sings from the same songbook." The larger the family, the more complex family conversations become, which is why the *practice of conversations* must be developed. The practice of conversation helps families prepare for the tough conversations before they arise.

Clarity in communication, open emotional expression, and collaborative problem solving are some of the characteristics of a healthy family—what Froma Walsh defines as "family resilience." According to Walsh, resilience involves a good communication process along with two other domains of family functioning: belief systems and organizational patterns.[10]

When differentiated successors transition the business culture from being egocentric to system-centric, they build resilience into the family. Egocentric mythologies cannot build a strong base for family functioning, because they tend to foster an ideology centered on one powerful individual who maintains tight control of the empire. The hero is strong and the family is weak.

In contrast to this, a strong family belief system serves as a credo and the source of its resilience—the heart and soul. According to Walsh, "Resilience is fostered by shared beliefs that increase the options for effective functioning, problem resolution, healing and growth." A belief system binds the family together while liberating the creative energies of its individuals. These beliefs unify the family in times of suffering when they influence the family view of and approach to crisis.

The organizational patterns of a resilient family are not the rigid, bureaucratic, and hierarchical grids typical of an egocentric system. Resilient family businesses are responsive and flexible, its members connected, with fluid roles, open feedback loops, and direct communication. They can quickly utilize social and economic resources at their disposal. To be resilient is to move forward the family legacy—and not the myth of the founder.

Next Generation

Chester Sykes, Jean Moran's father and founder of LMI Packaging Solutions, brought his 13-year-old grandson JP to the porch of his Door County beach home. "When we got there," JP recalls, "he gave me some things that were special to him(he was dying from cancer at the time), and then said, 'You're going to have to look after your mom [Jean]. Running the family business is going to be very tough on her. You need to watch out for her.' To this day I have never forgotten his words and do my best to live up to them."

As Jean Moran looked after her father, her son JP, the general manager of LMI Packaging Solutions, is looking after her. And his

---

[10]Froma Walsh, *Strengthening Family Resilience* (New York: The Guildford Press, 2006).

mother has ensured that he is equipped, along with his two sisters, to do so. Jean hired a leadership consultant to work with her three children, "to find their voices, make sure they are doing what they want to do, build their self-awareness, and above all to communicate and avoid the mistakes I made." Jean measures the success of the company by a triple bottom line: financial, social, and environmental, to which she expects all her children to contribute. "My one daughter has her own business," Jean says, "but she's really learning to work in our business."

Jean understands that mistakes are never final and rarely fatal. And she has learned the most from the ones she regrets the most, "all the family stuff," as she puts it. To Bill Wrigley's motto, "Respect the past ... " she offers this slight modification: "Learn from the past and do what's right for the future. And the future lies with the children."

FIRING A FAMILY MEMBER

The hardest thing that any family business successor can be faced with is to fire a family member. I mentioned previously that family businesses are an inherently enmeshed system. The values and rationale of the family, nurturing, equality, growth, and development are often intertwined with the business values of needing to hold an employee accountable for their performance. As a brother or sister, I want to support my siblings' growth and development, and don't want to cause them any pain. As a boss and as a leader, I am called to hold my employees accountable for the health of the business. Transparency, boundaries, and accountability are vital parts of a healthy system. When a family member is the employee that needs to be accountable, the successor is faced with a tension between the potential of creating conflict and resentment in the family by firing a family member and the negative impacts on the business of having a family employee who is not performing or is underperforming. Many successors have asked me, "How do you deal with this dilemma?"

Let's take the case of David, the youngest of three siblings. David was a high achiever and quickly showed himself to be a talented leader in the family hotel business. He quickly rose through the ranks and at the age of 35 was named as the successor to his father. This had a tremendous impact on David's older brother, Steve. Steve had been in the business longer than David, but had never really excelled. He had some moments of success, but after the announcement that David was going to lead the business, Steve's performance slowly slipped to the point where his decisions were costing the business money and creating resentment among the nonfamily employees.

David was faced with a dilemma. Do I risk alienating my brother and creating conflict, or do I do I hold my brother accountable and uphold the family value of hard work and good performance? While firing a family member is rarely if ever a smooth and unemotional process, the challenge is, how do I try to fulfill both the value of being a caring family member as well as the value of being a responsible leader?

The answer is to go through a process that not only addresses the performance of the family member but also engages them in a conversation about finding work and a role where they can be successful and happy. While being clear that low performance is not acceptable, you are also saying that as a sibling, parent, or cousin—I care about you as a family member and want the best for your future.

1. You need to have measures of performance that are clear and well known to the family employee.
2. You need to give clear and accurate feedback when a family member's performance is not sufficient.
3. As long as the family member's behaviors aren't egregious, they should have an adequate opportunity to address their performance.
4. If the family member's performance does not improve, then the conversation should shift to the question of how we as a family can help you find a job where you can be happy and successful, because that is what we as a family want for you. If the business can afford it, I recommend giving the family member time and support to find work that is meaningful to them and a role where they can be successful.

Firing a family member is never easy and will be an emotional experience regardless, but if you provide accountability, while also communicating that we love you and we want to help you find a place where you can be successful, you reduce the downside risk of dramatic family conflict.

CHAPTER

8

Me versus We

Sharing the glory of the family business story

Growing up, John Tyson's life was all chicken all the time.

After becoming chairman and CEO of the company in 2000, he, like his father and grandfather, led Tyson Foods through another period of dramatic expansion. In 2001, Tyson Foods became the world's largest processor and marketer of chicken, beef, and pork.

At a young age, there was no boundary between John's private life and his public one, as Tyson Foods and the Tyson family were one and the same.

The Tyson family was blended into the family of Tyson Foods, or Tyson Feed and Hatchery, as it was called at the time. At the age of 13, when most junior high boys roam the neighborhood with a pack of peers, John labored in the chicken factory alongside Tyson employees. "It's those people who raised me, not my dad. They were a gift; they allowed me to shape my own personality."

At an early age, John Tyson absorbed the notion that the Tyson family extended beyond his nuclear family. The people of Tyson Foods always mattered—and still matter—more than anything else. What John's father taught him was that Fridays were about making sure every employee was able to say, "Thank God, it's Friday." They had a paycheck. They were able to take care of their families. At the same time, the Tyson family said, "Thank God, we can make payroll."

"Monday's not hard," says John. "It's Friday when you have to make payroll [that's hard]. The emphasis and reemphasis was always on this large family that we called Tyson Foods."

In addition to what employees take home on Fridays, John cares about what they bring to work and what work gives to them beyond the paycheck. Work is a place where the workers don't stagnate. Growing the business means creating opportunities for people to grow. "How do you create an environment where folks who want to come along," says John, "have a chance to grow personally and professionally, and take care of their family? If we do that, then we create a culture of opportunity." For some, the opportunity is to leave the company, in the same way a child must leave home to grow up. "It's amazing the number of people I have fired," says John, "who have come back and said, 'If you hadn't fired me, I would have never gone and done what I wanted to do in life.'"

John says he views all his actions from the vantage point of responsibility, not personal fulfillment: "You've got to focus on what's right for every individual in the company.... I don't focus on what's right for me." His drug-and-alcohol addiction, for instance, was a personal failure, and his recovery was a "personal responsibility to all those who are counting on him." When he became sober, John accepted the job as steward of the Tyson brand: "Our responsibility is not to run Tyson Foods. The responsibility we've accepted is to organize a part of the agricultural chain to give folks a chance to buy a product at a fair price to feed their families."

The lines blur between who John Tyson is, what he does, and who he cares for—the extended Tyson family. He refuses, for example, to assume the title employees bestowed on his grandfather: the Good Chicken Man. "While he was widely known as a good businessman, he was better known as a Great Chicken Man." There was only one Chicken Man, and those who have succeeded John's grandfather have simply helped extend his vision to help folks put dinner on the table for their families.

This mindset, one of the markers that the family leader is on the journey of differentiation, is what Amway's Dick DeVos explains as the transition from a cult of personality to a set of ideals. One obvious and important way a successor does this is to focus on the people in the organization. Leaders who realize that their success depends on the people whom they lead refuse to indulge the cult of personality. Differentiated leaders diffuse the glory and take responsibility. "My advice to any successor in a family business," says John, "is to take care of your people first, because at the end of the road, the people will tell [you] what [you were]."

The "I" in the "We"

Taking care of people is a family business leader's highest calling, whether immediate family, relatives, or the employees who extend the family legacy. To do so, he or she must emerge from the shadows of a legendary parent, grandparent, or other family member. As I've argued in this book, the ongoing process of becoming a differentiated and generative leader begins with establishing credibility with his or her predecessor, and with family, shareholders, and stakeholders. A leader cannot support and care for employees without their respect and support.

How do leaders do that? They start with themselves. Building internal and external credibility starts with self-awareness. Self-awareness is to know one's self apart from who others say you are. It's recognizing one's humanity amidst the clamoring for a hero. It's a process that does not end upon succession, the ascension to power. In fact, the deeper insights of self-awareness often come long after a leader has established him- or herself.

Jean Moran's moment of insight came after years of leading LMI Packaging Solutions, when she realized that she wasn't leading the family business for the family but to be loved by her family. Only then was she able to truly do what was best for the organization as well as the family. Leaders who are not self-aware tend to have mono-vision: they see only themselves; their ego blinds them to the larger needs of the family and the employees whom they serve. When leaders seek to become a monolithic leader, they convince themselves that it's all on them. They refuse to see that they will need help on the journey, believing that success is solely of their making. That burden will crush them. Strong leaders understand that they don't have to do it all to prove it all to everybody. It's only then that leaders are truly free to serve, to feed the family, and to take care of their people.

Self-awareness triggers the process of differentiation. If self-awareness is to "know thyself" in relation to others, differentiation is to be okay with oneself in all the ways that he or she is different from others, especially the founder. For successors of family businesses, the process of differentiation doesn't cease upon transfer of leadership. Or, rather, it's not complete once the new leader rises to power. As a general rule, the more the predecessors have been mythologized, the more difficult it is to differentiate. Consequently, differentiation is more like a daily discipline, an ongoing grappling with becoming a unique leader, separate from the predecessor. Successors who achieve this can clarify what to hold on to (and therefore also reject) from the past in order to do what's best for the future.

Differentiated leaders are the eye in the storm, the point of stillness and self-control when emotions run amok around them. Where emotions obscure the exact nature of things, the differentiated leader is emotionally neutral so he or she can discern between the smokescreen and the fire within the organization. The undifferentiated leader responds to each emotion as if it is a crisis. The differentiated leader will approach more judiciously, and say, "Is there a problem attached to this emotion that I must solve, or is this person just upset because she isn't getting what she wants? If there is a problem, let's solve it. If not, then I need to get at the issue attending to this person's emotion." It's the classic difference between a thermometer and a thermostat. A thermometer reacts to the slightest change in temperature, and a thermostat sets the temperature around it. Because they have learned to manage their own emotions, good leaders can manage the emotional climate of their company.

Successors who are firmly grounded can look freely beyond the needs of their own ego to what the needs of the organization and its people are. When they aren't grounded, they resort to people pleasing and trying to tap down the emotion of those around them, rather than understand and deal with it.

This is critical for successors of a family business who need to separate themselves from a strong predecessor. They must communicate, "I am not my father." Or as John Tyson did, "I'm not the Good Chicken Man." Afraid to step out of the founder's shadow, some successors struggle to gain the respect and the support of the people, much less establish a culture where everyone feels like family. If the people see the successor merely seeking to copy the predecessor, they will have less respect for his or her ability to make quality decisions on his or her own.

The strongest leaders have a sense of the "I" in the "we." Knowing who they are and where they are going, their egos are not pulled apart by the competing demands of the people they lead. Their challenge is to increase a sense of common vision when people naturally want to accentuate their differences and compete. Leaders must change the way followers see themselves, from isolated individuals to members of a larger group. To do so, they must model commitment, reinforce collective goals, share corporate values, and create coherence around a vision. A leader forges unity.

The rallying point for unity is a clear vision, which leaders communicate in ordinary ways every time they talk with anyone in their organization. And they never stop talking about it. In this way, leaders share ownership of the vision with the people and reinforce that they are key contributors to its success. The family teaches the values and engages the employees in an inspiring vision.

From Legendary to Ordinary

Generative successors who hardwire longevity into their family business have a genuine sense of humility that comes from being grounded. They stay humble, as strange as that sounds, in a world of personalities and personal branding. Their humility and accessibility tend to demythologize the legends. They avoid the trap of grandiosity formed by an egocentric mythology, which feeds the delusion that it's a one-man show. This, in fact, only perpetuates a leader's isolation from his people. Leaders step out from behind the curtain and reveal who they truly are. And they know their employees. They understand the impact of what each employee does and its contribution to the larger goal.

Differentiated leaders have the humility to discern the strengths of others around them, and they have developed a deep appreciation for their contributions to the success of the business. They hone their ability to get "the right people on the bus." They have firsthand knowledge of what their employees are doing because they regularly get out of the office. They are willing to get their hands dirty, whatever that means in the business. They learn to speak the language of the laborer. Mary Andringa of the Vermeer Corporation remembers her father as a man of the people, who loved talking with employees. "He had messages that hit home with people," she says. "My dad loved to go to job sites and get out in the field. When he was among the people, he was real. You can't ever underestimate how important it is to be there in the flesh, on the shop floor, to shake the people's hands, to tell them thanks for what they do. I learned from him to be hands-on, out and about and not in my office."

When a leader stands in the trenches with the men and women who work for her business, she wins their devotion. A business is built in the same way a battle is won: at the front, with those in the trenches. Bill Wrigley traveled deep into the Indonesian jungle to visit families tapping rubber trees for Wrigley Spearmint Gum. He recalls a trip to Sumatra, riding with two other men on a rickety railroad track with gutted support beams. "We stuffed ourselves into this cart used to transport rubber, and one guy draped himself over my shoulders while the other guy kicked every third railroad tie to propel us. We picked up a head of steam and rode right into the jungle. All of a sudden, this family of Wrigley employees comes out of a tent, and it was like the Martians had just beamed in. For 15 minutes, we talked in the language of smiles while they showed us their camp. I finally understood the worldwide effort to put one piece of gum in my mouth."

It took being out in the field for Bill to also understand its impact on his employees. "There is nothing like being on the ground with someone, and especially breaking bread with them—it's a bond you create with them wherever they are. Those people will still walk through walls for me, just for spending that time."

There is a direct relationship between the health of the business and health and happiness of its employees. Financial packages and corporate perks are far less important than employee well-being. Research shows that family CEOs make less money than nonfamily CEOs, and private-company CEOs make less than public CEOs. In many cases, there's less emotional inflation of salaries, with financial compensation tied to the reality of what's happening on the ground.[1] Money in well-run family businesses tends to be more equally distributed, without extreme disparities in employee salaries.

When the Magnetic Center Is Gone

A successful family business is created by the vision of its founder. To survive across generations, the vision must outlast him. If a leader's personality is the centrifugal force of the business, it may stop when he or she does. As Dick DeVos says, "When a personality dies, the magnetic center is gone," and the business often falls apart.

To create a sustainable organization, a leader must maintain a network of talented people who are loyal to a vision (what the leader stood for), not a personality (who the leader is). The founding

---

[1]Anderson and Reeb, "Founding Family Ownership and Firm Performance: Evidence from the S&P 500," *Journal of Finance* 58(3) (2003): 1301–1328.

fathers of the United States drafted a vision statement that distilled the best of America's dreams. It is the Constitution that we uphold, not the people who framed it. This vision has sustained the United States as a world leader from generation to generation. In a similar way, a family business vision carries the family values and helps the business to grow beyond the mythological image of its founder. It creates opportunities for generations to come. It is the generative successor that taps into this and builds on it.

A differentiated leader is also humble enough to serve his or her own vision, and has the foresight to be a steward of the brand and not its lord. As Christie Hefner, former chairwoman and chief executive officer of Playboy Enterprises, says, "I considered my role to be a steward of a brand, of a culture, of shareholders, of employees. I had an obligation to serve those masters." Because she had a long-term stake in the brand, Christie says, "I had an emotional stake in the people. This helped people ... support me and follow me." A visionary leader puts systems in place that do not allow egos to run unchecked, starting with his or her own. The leader is the first person to serve the system.

One thing that makes us human (mortal) is the yearning to serve something larger than the self, and the ability to resist our impulses in favor of some larger purpose. The leader models a culture where what's good for the group trumps self-interest. Self-interested employees are more interested in looking good and getting promoted than in helping the company.

Feels Like Family

If corporate culture can be defined in layperson terms as "what it's like to work around here," the ultimate compliment from an employee is, "It feels like family here." It's a cliché, except when it's reality. Successful family businesses weave the founding family values into the fabric of the business.

Family values are the soul of the business and create the business culture in which each individual feels like he or she is essential to the fabric of the company. But at the same time, there is an environment of accountability to each other, the mission, and the vision. Under the umbrella of values, employees feel cared for like family. They feel empowered. They show initiative, creativity, and leadership within their sphere of influence. And they believe their voices can make a difference in how the company is run. They are held accountable for their actions and performance.

In many companies, employees are often valued more as a commodity than a person of influence. The irony is that the people are a company's source of creativity and innovation. A leader can't inspire a machine. But when people are inspired, they feel valued. And when people are valued, they become valuable. This is the wellspring of energy that a successor can tap into.

Family businesses don't exist solely for money. If the goal were only money, they would take the business public or sell the business, and when the wire hits the bank, they would do something else. Many family-owned businesses would say its assets are what's on the balance sheet, but their wealth is their relationships, their reputation, and what they give to the community. Because of this, family-owned businesses tend to value people, not just the company assets. They don't see employees as merely a number or a budget line. They are quicker to understand the human reality of corporate downsizing and are slower to lay off in down times.[2] Family businesses invest more in resources and training.[3] Perhaps born out of a sense of personal responsibility, generative family business successors take better care of their people as an asset of the company.

More like primary-care physicians than specialists, family business owners tend to be more in tune with their employees' overall well-being than their counterparts in publicly held firms. Many are quick to address employee groaning, optimize employee strengths, and reward employee contributions. In short, they commit to employees, and, as a result, tend to hold on to employees longer.[4]

Family business is not just about the bloodline but also about the lifeblood of the organization: employees. They are the reason a family business succeeds in a roiling economy and its mission reaches the community. Often, employees are loyal from generation to generation. One way that successors of family businesses build this loyalty is by pushing down decision making as far as they can through the organizational structure. By doing so, people on the front line attach what they do to the mission and vision of the business.

---

[2]Mass Mutual/Raymond Institute American Family Business Survey, 2003.

[3]D. Miller and I. LeBreton-Miller, *Managing for the Long Run* (Boston: Harvard Business School Press, 2005).

[4]Ibid.

Small businesses tend to do this much better than large corporations. Large corporations use a series of institutionalized carrots and sticks (usually, a combination of policies, procedures, and monetary rewards) to motivate employees to act in a way the company desires. People are drawn to status and a paycheck rather than to the values of the organization. This is the classic climb up the corporate ladder: Success is measured by how high up the ladder one goes, along with increasing monetary rewards at each rung. Large corporations are people-challenged, because, with exceptions, they tend to treat people as a commodity. Employees then tend to feel less ownership of their jobs, and, consequently, their unique contribution to the corporate mission. Employment becomes a transaction: my work for your pay.

A differentiated leader elicits the opposite response from employees. It's a kind of leadership that activates pride, loyalty, and enthusiasm about the mission and vision of the organization. The almost paternalistic feel of working for the family elicits a feeling of being cared for. Employees receive a sense of emotional return as they work to add to the financial return. Regardless of role, title, or position, employees who feel they are part of something great will contribute to making the company greater. This approach to leadership generates social capital—the bonds of trust that hold a hard-working community together. Trust comes from listening, reflecting, and communicating that each person is valued in the organization. When people feel valued, status and salary are still important but not primary. A great leader enjoys talking with a truck driver as much as she likes talking with her COO. To value employees is to listen to them. As Chester Sykes put it in the mission statement for Label Makers, Inc. (now LMI Packaging Solutions), "This is a place where employees have a voice."

Differentiated leaders understand that people respond and perform better when they are intrinsically motivated. I liken intrinsic motivation to internal credibility, the degree to which a person feels he or she has value.

In his *New York Times* best seller, *Drive*, Daniel Pink explores the reality of what motivates people at work.[5] While exploring this theme, Pink looks at the traditional carrot-and-stick approach to motivating

---

[5]Daniel H. Pink, *Drive: The Surprising Truth about What Motivates Us* (New York: Riverhead Books, 2011).

people. He found that while the approach might work for simple tasks, it doesn't work for the more complex tasks that most employees are engaged in every day. Pink found that to motivate people in complex tasks, leaders must give them *autonomy, mastery,* and *purpose*: all things that family businesses are well positioned to provide. If leaders want engagement from people, they give them autonomy, the freedom and space to do their job. Mastery is the desire to get better at something that is meaningful to us. A sense of purpose comes from the vision of the family and aligning our talents and expertise with what the system needs.

Through a focus on their people, generative successors create an environment of trust with their employees and give them the autonomy to do their jobs. As John Tyson sees his goal as providing opportunity for his people, the generative successor delights in seeing their people build skills and improve at what they do. And, finally, the vision that they cast gives to their employees a sense of meaning and purpose to their work.

I believe that family businesses are better positioned than any other economic or commercial institution to provide intrinsic motivation. Businesses build value by prioritizing the value of people, and helping them feel valuable.

More than Money

"Money talks, but it don't sing and dance and it don't walk." American singer-songwriter Neil Diamond tells us why the dollar is not almighty. Money rewards people, but it doesn't celebrate them. What employees need is more basic and more powerful than money. It's the recognition that they are valuable, they belong, and their contribution makes a difference. Leaders reward people with money; they celebrate people with recognition.

A CEO doesn't rally his people by talking about what he or she is doing for them. He shares the glory. Generative successors embody *Level 5 leadership,* a term coined by Jim Collins in his bestseller *Good to Great.* They "channel their ego needs away from themselves and into their larger goal of building a great company."[6] Generative successors think first of the family business system and not themselves.

---

[6]Jim Collins, *Good to Great* (New York: Harper Collins, 2001).

Nothing inspires a group more than the story of a common person who embodies the business's values and inspires everyone else to uphold those values. Leaders talk about success by celebrating the people who make the right things happen, or prevent the wrong things from happening. Small or big, it doesn't matter, because it all matters.

A leader asks, "Do we recognize the people who help us solve problems and create opportunities?" as well as, "Are we intentional about celebrating those contributions?" There are practical and structural ways leaders can do this, like awards programs. A family I work with invested in an awards program that revolves around the company's seven values. Every year, employees nominate each other to receive awards for upholding the values in some way. The family leaders not only reinforce their seven values, but they also celebrate an eighth tacit value: the people who demonstrate the other seven. Along with the recognition come the stories of what these employees have done.

Telling a collective tale of what the business is accomplishing together is one way of sharing the success of the family business. It also staves off the creation of a mythology of the successor. Media celebrate the monolithic leader. Humans want a hero, someone that they can connect with. And it's simpler to tell a story of a hero than the heroic feats of many. Though more complex to tell, the stories that celebrate supporting players are richer because they reflect a group that has cumulatively sacrificed for the greater good of the organization's mission. Humble leaders avoid the trap of narcissistic grandiosity and share the credit with others.

Leaders cannot develop this sense of humility without differentiating—the process by which they have developed internal and external credibility. The undifferentiated leader is happy to be the hero the press is clamoring for. The accolades stoke an ego beleaguered by insecurity. However, the hero story alienates family members and employees. Undifferentiated successors subtly allow a new family business myth that creates a shadow for the next generation. In contrast, differentiated leaders look for ways to share the glory and take responsibility for failures. They understand that people are valuable to the organization when they are valued. One of the best ways a successor can create unity around his vision is to let his people be the heroes of the success stories.

Dream Weaver

But stories aren't enough. A leader must also tap into his people's deepest imaginations, the place that spawns their dreams for the future. The family business is not just a place to put in a good day's work; it's a place that kindles people's imagination, encourages them to dream, and helps their dreams come true. The best leaders want those dreams to become part of a company's ongoing story. They look for ways to weave those dreams into the larger vision.

Dream work is advanced-level leadership. The leader has already demonstrated a commitment to employees when he or she encourages them to take ownership and pride in what they do for the business. But helping people achieve their own dreams is the ultimate proof that they are valued. It encourages them to take ownership of their lives, and gives them hope for a better future (sometimes apart from the organization).

Mike Hamra, CEO of Hamra Enterprises, has developed a "Dream Manager program" and placed a "Dream Manager" in charge. The program encourages employees to articulate their dreams, everything from "I want to run a marathon" to "I want to own a house" to "I want to work in the fashion industry." The Dream Manager looks at how the organization can help them make it happen.

Dream work acknowledges that a business dreams along with its people. Leaders recognize that the business improves as its people live into their dreams. But the genius of Hamra's program is that it tells people that their dreams start *now*, so that they become more passionate and feel more connected to what they are doing *now*. These are not "beautiful dreamers" who look out the window when they should be working. These are industrious dreamers who engage in their work because they know it is work that makes their dreams attainable.

Mike Hamra trains competence and confidence so that his people know they can get another job if that is their dream. He doesn't want people staying at a job with Hamra Enterprises because they are afraid they can't do anything else. He wants them on fire.

The Brick Wall

In family-owned businesses, the emerging leader often struggles with credibility, as I've argued through this book. Successors typically hit two kinds of walls: the wall of their own insecurity and the wall of family resistance. Some leaders feel insecure when they inherit the crown. If they feel they didn't earn their title, they may look for ways to prove themselves, sometimes taking credit when others deserve the credit, as I've already discussed. This is classic image management. They waste energy crafting an image of credibility as a leader. Invariably, the attempt backfires. People can smell out insecurity and the inauthentic attempt to mask it.

Fearful leaders preoccupied with image management shut down on their people. They isolate themselves, stop listening, and try to consolidate power rather than empower their employees and bring out the best in them. A leader's greatest asset—the leadership team and employees—then becomes a liability, but only because a leader projects his or her insecurities on them. In reality, the people are not the problem. The leader is.

Most families of family-owned businesses are committed to their people. However, in times of crisis, when a leader's strength is most needed, an insecure leader generates fear instead of trust. Fear intensifies misperceptions and distorts reality.

Trust is the family currency. When it is depleted, a family starts to eat away at its assets and compromise its values. It will abandon the commitment to the philosophy that its people are the business's greatest asset. When differentiated leaders hit the double wall of insecurity and family resistance, they bounce off and redirect. If they can't move the wall, they move themselves: "Maybe it's time that I shift." The shift is from victimhood to ownership. Mike Hamra tried to push his dad out of the business. Yet when he realized his dad needed to be connected to the business in some way, he was able to make the shift to "OK, well maybe I need to shift to figure out how to keep him connected to the business in a productive way." That type of shifting is helpful to the business long term.

Re-Generation

The family (not the business) is the golden goose, and the goose must reproduce. A differentiated successor has the long view. He or she does not lead merely to maximize value for the current generation. It is easy to engineer short-term financial success. The work of generativity is to generate both financial and emotional returns to its stakeholders over time, not just for this generation, but the next.

Differentiated leaders recognize that the family business is an asset and desire to leave the organization better than when they received it from the previous generation. They embrace the task of passing on a legacy apart from a cult of personality.

Christie Hefner had to separate herself from the cult of "the Hef" when she took over leadership from her father at Playboy Enterprises in the 1980s. The Hef's man-about-town celebrity was a press feeding frenzy. In the backdrop, Christie managed tough business decisions, like deciding which Playboy enterprises to shut down. "In those early days," she says, "the company was in trouble." But Christie refused to let the trouble topple the family legacy. "I cared about the long-term health of the company. It was the antithesis of what was happening in the early 80s: a company got in trouble, the board hired Chainsaw Al who would parachute in and cut lots of jobs, cut lots of investment spending, collect a huge bonus, and be gone in four years." In caring about the long-term health of the company, Christie cared for employees.

This was the cornerstone of her credibility. Christie says, "True power is given by the people you lead, not by the people who gave you the job. To exercise leadership and power, people have to be willing to follow you. You have to work really hard to get people to tell you what they really think, because the combination of power and family business can be deadly in terms of people trying to just figure out what you want them to say."

If as Christie says, true power is given by the people, then the best thing an emerging leader can do to build credibility is to become a good listener, invest in the leadership team and employees, and begin thinking now about the next generation. Caring for the long-term health of the business means caring for employees today.

CHAPTER 9

Decisions, Decisions

Decisiveness amidst ambiguity

Technology waits for no one, not even revered and legendary institutions.

In 1995, the iconic Crane & Co., manufacturer of fine stationery paper and US currency paper since 1879, faced looming obsolescence. Between 1950 and the 1980s, the company, led by the fifth generation of the Crane family, produced a range of highly successful products, including drafting paper, stock certificate paper, carbon paper, and business stationery. Then technology changed radically, and Crane & Co.'s business slowed almost to a standstill.

The copy machine and e-mail (now dated technology) rendered many of their products obsolete. In addition, competitors vied for their almost 100-year-old contract with the US government for whom they made currency paper.

Stymied, Crane & Co.'s summoned Lansing Crane, the great-great-great grandson of the company's founder, Zenas Crane. Lansing was in the full bloom of his career, practicing law and teaching courses in psychiatry and law at Yale. But the call came, and, as he says, "It was time for me to come home to the family business."[1] The family business to which he returned is steeped in American history. In 1776, Stephen Crane had combined water, horsepower, and heat with worn-out cotton rags collected from local housewives to produce paper at Liberty Mill, just outside Boston. He sold his

[1] Kelly Cunningham, "Good on Paper," *Bostonia* (Fall 2006).

product to engraver Paul Revere, who printed on it the Colonies' first banknotes. Crane & Co. made cotton the fabric of Americans' lives by recycling it into paper: greeting cards, invitations, wedding announcements, and banknotes.

"The paper has to feel good," says Lansing. "The other part of our identity is the distinctive feel that goes with the finest paper you can buy. There's a pleasure and a quality of life that goes with fine paper."[2] Reflecting on his early experiences of Crane & Co., Lansing assigns an almost mythological quality to the mills where the paper was produced. "Growing up, I would go into the paper mills with my father, who was head of manufacturing," says Lansing. "Skids of paper standing around, the paper machines moving along—it was a fascinating thing for a young boy. More than that, there was warmth and a relationship between the people in the mills and our family that I observed and appreciated even as a child."[3] Lansing understands his work to be "a labor of love" and an opportunity to add his small part to the family legacy.

His small part was actually a pivotal role. He changed Crane & Co.'s core competencies while preserving its values and history. Lansing came into the company as an outsider with an insider's credentials. His respect for Crane & Co.'s values was matched by a fresh perspective. The board followed his lead away from the paper trail they had blazed for two centuries to pioneer a new venture that incorporated a micro-optic security thread called "Motion" into the paper bills. "Motion" threads, blue-green strips that create an optical illusion of images sliding in directions perpendicular to the light that catches them, are essential components to high-value banknotes across the world. They are "a watershed security feature," Lansing says.

Lansing did what few leaders can do: He turned a threat into an opportunity. The technology that exposed the vulnerabilities of the business helped transform his family's domestic paper company into an international technology company and a leader in the global currency market. "Our journey into an international business necessarily drove change in our company's culture and practices, reinvigorating

---

[2]Ibid.
[3]Ibid.

us into one functioning and integrated company,"[4] Lansing says. In other words, he took risks, and they paid off.

He made two big decisions that stretched the company far outside its comfort zone of a distinctly American family business. The first decision in 2001 was to buy the Tumba Bruk print and paper subsidiary from Sweden's Central Bank to establish an international platform and diversify the company. The diversification required recruitment of new talent outside the company, forcing a global mentality and a mini family migration. Four Crane employees moved to Sweden to help run the Swedish division of 1,500 employees. Lansing's second decision to invest in the development of "Motion" thread led to Crane's purchase in 2008 of Nanoventions, an Atlanta-based security tech company, which gave Crane & Co. exclusive control of the micro-optic security technology used in banknote manufacturing. It also gave sustainable competitive advantage to Crane in the international banknote business. "Motion" thread is now the dominant security feature in the US $100 bill and the currency of many other countries

Lansing's decisions forced the company to change, learn new skills, and define success in a way it had never done before. While it would be romantic to say that there was no resistance to these changes, the reality is that resistance surrounded Lansing. He had to deal with resistance from both long-time employees and family alike. But, remaining steadfast to his vision for what needed to change, Lansing's bold moves gave the family business a future in the global banknote business—a growing, high-value market. Those decisions have also made the internal fabric of Crane & Co. as strong as the paper it continues to print, which lasts four times longer than any other world currency. While Lansing drove the process, an enduring legacy of Yankee ingenuity and resilience propelled the organization. "Yankee values have served us well over generations, and I hope will continue to. Humility should be part of any ownership culture and worldview, underscored by the philosophy that there are no fingerprints on success. The success of

---

[4]Paul Karofsky, "More than Making Money: How Crane and Company Used Legacy Values to Transform an Iconic American Brand," *FFI Intelligence Matters: Strategies for Family Enterprise Success* (2009), www.ffi.org.

a business is truly a collective act—one neither the family alone nor any individual can take credit for."[5]

The Great Differentiator

The hallmark of the differentiated leader is the ability to make decisions that push the company forward into unknown territory at critical moments in a company's history. Tough decisions are gut checks, especially when the prosperity of the family business is dependent on the decision being right. The right decision isn't always guaranteed, of course. Strong leaders are decisive, even when the outcome isn't guaranteed. Leaders who abdicate their role in making crucial decisions become a liability to the business. The business can't move forward if the leader isn't moving forward. Decisions reveal a leader, and demonstrate how successfully he or she has differentiated from the founder, or in the case of Lansing Crane, five generations of successors who followed the founder.

Lansing Crane used his values to make gutsy decisions and move Crane & Company forward into the twenty-first century. In doing so, he differentiated his leadership from that of previous generations. For many successors, differentiation happens as they find their way *in* the family business. However, for Lansing, differentiation began outside the family business. Lansing studied law but developed expertise in psychiatry. While teaching both at Yale, he drafted legislation protecting the rights of psychiatric patients in Connecticut. His perceived outsider-insider perspective proved to be an asset. "It was because I had done something different from other Crane family members that the family elders felt that I could add something."[6] Lansing understates the urgency of that call, and the nature of his differences. In reality, the company was floundering and it needed an insider with an outside perspective—someone who could stand in the gap between what the company had been and what it needed to become. Someone who was credible in his own right and had credibility with others and could see the bigger picture.

We are all faced with the task of differentiation, the process of developing the ability to stand in the presence of emotion and stay in command of our decision making. But the task morphs into a bigger

---

[5] Ibid.

[6] Ibid.

challenge in a family business with a storied history. Family mythology, as I have argued to this point, can weigh heavily on a successor. In Crane & Co., it wasn't the mythology of just a founder, it was the weight and legacy of generations of the company that threatened to engulf the next family leader. For Lansing Crane, the burden was lessened because he differentiated outside the family business. Having some separation from the family business allowed him to develop his sense of self, separate from the family. While the task at hand wasn't any easier, he had a sense of confidence that was based on what he accomplished apart from the influence of the five generations that preceded him. Simply, he became his own man before he entered the business.

Decisions are the steps a successor takes as he or she walks out of the shadows of a legendary founder. They reveal a leader's self-awareness, experience, and knowledge, as well as his or her clarity of vision and values. If these are muddled by the shadows of the founder, the way forward is often unclear. When Lansing came home to Crane & Co, he was able to lead the organization, informed by the collective wisdom and experience of the board, and having a strong sense of his own credibility from a long track record of success.

Once formed, people's self-concepts are an important source of input to their decisions. Lansing's outside career accomplishments helped form self-esteem and establish his reputation (external credibility) to make the right decisions at a critical juncture in Crane & Co.'s history. In making those decisions, Lansing leveraged the mythology of the Crane brand (its "emotional meaning to Americans over many generations"[7]) while harnessing technology to augment the company's core products on a global scale. "Our move into the international market was a big deal for us," he says. "It requires more talent and focus, has made us more competitive, and has increased our level of diversification. It's reinforced the company's strengths. I think my predecessors in the family would have understood that and been excited about it, as we are."

Cutting the Gordian Knot

In 1879, the US Treasury, dissatisfied with its currency paper supplier, put its contract out for bid. On May 27 of that year, Winthrop

---

[7] Ibid.

Murray Crane—a future US senator—sent a telegram to the Crane home office from Washington, DC: "You must let me use my judgment about changing the bid . . . . No time to spare."

"They already had the bids in," says Lansing Crane. "He went in at the last minute and bid one-fourth of a penny below the next-lowest bid. We'd never made the paper before, and we weren't sure we could."[8] But Crane & Co. got the contract.

To decide is to act, and to decide wisely is to act decisively, making informed decisions without being impulsive or reckless. All the leadership traits that we have looked at so far—building credibility, becoming self-aware, learning through trial and error, building values, articulating a vision—are wrapped into the larger task of differentiation. The undifferentiated leader is more likely to be swayed by emotion, others' opinions of them, and their own fear of failure. By contrast, the differentiated leader acts more decisively. The decision becomes the tip of the sword that cuts the Gordian knot. Differentiation says, "I have inherited all of these from the family, but I have made them mine. I bear the family coat of arms but also leave my distinct imprint. I am proud of my family but also of my unique contribution. I have added value."

In the end, though, it's testing that proves leadership. The acid test is when the leader is called to make tough personal decisions. A differentiated leader manages both the emotion and the data. He or she works to understand and balance the needs of both the family and the business. The generative successor knows when the business needs to sacrifice for the family and when the family needs to sacrifice for the business. Lansing, for instance, had to fire some family members. At this point, "The business comes first," he says. A decision that would put considerable strain on his relationships with both siblings and cousins needed to be made for the long-term health of the family business system.

Vision tells a company where it's headed; values keep it on course; and, decisions get it there. At a point of crisis, a successor earns the right to lead by taking decisive action to create a new way forward. In "The Tests of a Prince," Ivan Lansberg writes, "The history of every family company that survived for generations tells us

---

[8]Kelly Cunningham, "Good on Paper," Bostonia (Fall 2006) P. 34–27.

of heroic feats at decisive moments that consolidated the authority of untested successors."[9]

These are defining decisions that employees, shareholders, and family members look for in a successor, a leader who acts decisively from his own conviction. This is especially the case when there is no clear way forward, and a leader must build a bridge across a chasm of uncertainty. It calls for creativity and innovation—and calculated risk.

While we would like to think that a leader always knows exactly what to do, but often the way forward is unclear. "You have to be able to take risks—not crazy risks, but risks," Crane says. "At key points in Crane's history, we've taken risks, and it's paid off. We stayed vibrant. We survived. That's how. Also, we don't ever get too far from our old-fashioned values: integrity, quality, honesty."[10] Risk involves being able to deal with ambiguity. It is rare that a leader has 100 percent certainty in making a decision. Generative successors have the capacity to deal with the ambiguity and not be overcome with anxiety. They neither rush to a decision, nor do they succumb to the paralysis of analysis. They make a decision and learn from it. Innovators are not imitators. They respect the past and are grounded in its values, but they can make a new way when the situation calls for it.

It's the difference between being reactive and proactive. The reactive approach to ambiguity is, "I am going to do what my parents did. I'm going to do what everybody else defines as success." The proactive approach is, "I'm going back to my value system and choosing the best course of action that fulfills my mission, leads me towards my vision, and is consistent with my values."[11]

One Decision after Another

Good leaders make decisions that assure that their organizations move in a purposeful direction. A proactive leader makes decisions and learns from them. A good decision can be reinforced by another, and a bad decision can be corrected by a good one. It's a long

---

[9]Ivan Lansberg, "The Tests of a Prince," *Harvard Business Review* (September 2007).

[10]Kelly Cunningham, "Good on Paper," Bostonia (Fall 2006) P. 34–27.

[11]Ibid.

progression in the same direction. Big decisions are rarely precipitous or fortuitous; rather, they tend to be deliberate and slow, requiring thought and strategic planning, because they set the long-term course of a growing company. Leaders need both the fast thinking of intuition and slow thinking of logic and collective wisdom.

Lansing Crane's decision to invest in the "Motion" technology required years of adapting the company's core technology to banknotes. And it followed the earlier decision to buy the Swedish Tumba Bruk paper and print subsidiary from Sweden's Central Bank. Smaller decisions reinforce the big ones, keeping the company on course. Making both kinds of decisions, big and small, is a learned skill, and the only way a leader learns to make decisions is by making them.

Failure Makes the Business Hero

Successors develop the ability to make good decisions when parents give them opportunities to make decisions early on, well before they are thrust into senior leadership roles. It starts small when the risk is low and the capacity for learning is high. This can happen naturally and with minimal pressure, when children start to "hang around" the workplace with their parents. Parents can capitalize on their curiosity by first giving children small tasks and then meaningful tasks involving decisions. Dick DeVos started by moving boxes in the basement. Mary Andringa's father gave her the controls of his Piper Cub airplane when she was 14, and Mary had her pilot's license three years later. "You will figure it out," said Jean Moran's father. When she figured it out, her self-confidence soared, and her father gave her bigger tasks.

Successors prematurely pushed onto the big stage of leadership are exposed. They can't fake it. Successors who make big decisions before they have learned the decision-making process often make poor decisions. The fault is often that their family has idealized them. As Massimo Ferragamo says, "Idealizing a child is not ideal for the business."

I have described the process of idealization as exaggerating positive qualities in a person. Idealization provides the illusion of perfection, and idealized children are perfect to a fault, and then to a failure. They are not given the opportunity to learn and develop their gut in the real world of trial and error. Protecting a child from this, a parent sets up his or her child for failure as an adult. As adults, when they make decisions that will inevitably fail, they often lack the fortitude and confidence to learn from the failure. That failure translates into, "I am a failure," because they have not learned to differentiate their real self from their idealized self, who is seemingly immune to failure.

In some cases, a successor who has been idealized grows an inflated sense of self. The story these successors wrongly believe is that they can do no wrong. Take Peter (not his real name). Peter was the first-born son of Lawrence Haubt. Lawrence was a creative visionary who very much wanted to see his son, Peter, and daughter, Mary, run the furniture manufacturing business that he had built. The business had become known as one of the most creative luxury furniture businesses in the world. Peter had a very gregarious and outgoing personality, was a hard worker, and was liked by all; however, his track record with the company was spotty at best. The fact that Peter was well liked caused Lawrence to overlook much of Peter's poor performance at all levels of the company. In fact, he never held his son accountable for his performance. So when Lawrence stepped back from leadership, handing the reins of the company to a 28-year-old, Peter had no grounding in who he was. He thought he was infallible. It wasn't until several of his decisions threatened the future of the company that his father developed a real sense of his son's ability. Lawrence stepped back in, but at a huge emotional cost to his son's self-esteem.

If accountability had started at a much earlier age, perhaps Peter and the family would have been spared the trauma of removing Peter as CEO.

Trap of Perfectionism

When a leader is caught up in her own mythology, she avoids decisions that might shatter her heroic stature.

This is the trap of perfectionism. The desire for perfection is rooted deep in our psyche, and our mythologies bear this out. All cultures have stories of the mythic leader (the king archetype we discussed earlier) that reveal our desire for a sovereign who brings order to chaos, and makes our world right.

These large stories are written small in all our lives, and successors continue the archetypal pattern when they celebrate and portray leaders as fearless, brilliant, and almost flawless. These legendary founders always made the right call, the "perfect decision." But the real world doesn't work that way. Rarely, if ever, does a leader make a perfect decision.

Vulnerable leaders, as we have seen, have the courage to be imperfect and to make decisions that reveal their vulnerability, not their invincibility. Mistakes are how they learn. Vulnerable leaders also have the strength to sit in ambiguity, when a decision they have made does not bear immediate and successful results. Certainty is safer than ambiguity, but it closes the door to the "what-ifs": "What if we do it this way?" "What if we try this?" A successor who does not have a strong sense of self, and has not pursued differentiation, will settle for the "what I know." He will play it safe, but will also remove the opportunity of ambiguity, the creative struggle to work through it. Often, it is from the creative struggle that an organization's greatest discoveries and innovations are born. Brene Brown, author of *Daring Greatly*, asserts that our greatest creativity and innovation comes from a place of vulnerability.[12] A leader who has not learned to be vulnerable and to be comfortable with ambiguity will never break through.

A differentiated leader is confident enough to make a call—even if it's the wrong one—because he is less concerned with sustaining a cult of personality than with doing what is right for the business. He isn't worried about how a wrong decision will hurt his image. But he is worried about making a decision that is in the best interest of the organization. These leaders understand that you don't always get it right. Some ideas work, some flop. They use a foundation of values and their sense of mission and vision as their guide.

At the end of a failure, a successor comes to a fork in the road and can either take the path of defeat or the path of instruction. To learn from defeat, however, a leader must be humble. Differentiated leaders are humble enough to learn from their mistakes, and strong enough to grow from them. Failure is part of that trial-and-error process. It gives us data to use as we seek to improve and grow. An undifferentiated leader is more likely to attribute failure to something being wrong with him, rather than saying, "I failed. So what? Move on."

---

[12]Brene Brown, *Daring Greatly: How the Courage to Be Vulnerable Transforms the Way We Live, Love, Parent, and Lead* (New York: Gotham Books, 2012).

Think and Do: The Decision-Making Process

John Tyson went to college, but he went to school at work. As he said, "They don't teach you business at a business school." Perhaps that's because students tend to not make many real-life decisions at school. You can't mimic the pressure of meeting payroll; you can't simulate the pressure of making decisions that impact the lives of hundreds of families. Decisions reveal what a leader has learned, and they help a leader learn more. "To learn to make decisions, you must have a thought process," says Tyson. "Have a good thought process; make a decision. Two things happen when you make a decision. It's right and you go faster, or it's wrong and you stop and make another decision."

Good thinking and good decisions reinforce each other to create action. It's the opposite of a self-fulfilling prophecy in which a false belief reinforces self-defeating behavior. Decisions test the soundness of the thought: Is it grounded in reality and experience? Leaders don't shy away from this process, because they have developed confidence from having made enough of the right calls in previous situations.

They are not afraid of doing the wrong thing, because they know that mistakes are both instructive and most often correctible. As John Tyson says, "If the feedback says, 'No, it's not right,' then stop, make another decision right then and there." The best leaders are not after perfection but progress. And they don't seek to be always right, but more right than wrong. Their thought process and intuition are reliable guides in situations that call for decisive action to move a company forward.

Must-Have Courage

Jean Moran was at the crossroads of a drastic decision. Keep a $5 million client happy, or prove the service that typified her company to a much smaller client.

Jean's company, LMI Packaging Solutions, was one of three smaller companies that serviced the much larger Winpak Portion Packaging, one of the country's largest suppliers of coffee creamers. When Jean asked for more of its business, Winpak rebuffed her every time. It was their intention to keep all three of their suppliers close in volume.

That's when temptation came knocking. One of Winpak's customers, whom LMI was not currently serving, needed a product that

Winpak did not want to provide. Winpak, the lowest-cost producer of a similar product, did not want to bastardize their existing business and so refused to give it to them.

"Can you supply us?" they asked Jean.

"Although we didn't have exactly what they needed, I said, 'Of course we can.' All it would take was a little creativity."

Jean had a good relationship with Winpak and asked straight up if LMI Packaging could give this other company what it needed, since Winpak did not want to. When Winpak said no, "we had a decision to make," says Jean. "That is, I had a decision to make, and I decided to take this client's business." When Winpak's VP of sales called Jean to tell her to back down, she responded, "I will, if you let me supply what they need." When he refused, Jean told him that LMI was going to do it anyway.

Three months later, the president of Winpak, who was a close friend and mentor to Jean, came to her office and fired LMI as a vendor. "As soon as he left the room," Jean says, "I pumped my fist in the air, and yelled out, 'YES!' like some psychotic."

The reaction belied her true feelings. She had just caused the company to lose a long-time customer who represented one third of their business. But bolstered by her own bravado, Jean called a meeting to inform her leadership team of the decision. "I was rah-rah-rah, we can do this" she laughs. "I had their full support. They trusted me."

It was only later that Jean found out that she had made the right decision. Winpak was a $5 million client with a 5 percent margin; the new client was only a $2 million client, but with a 40 percent margin. It was a difference of $550,000 to the bottom line.

Jean Moran trusted her instincts even as her more rational mind waved a red flag. She weighed all the factors and made a judgment call even when she did not have all the information (as we rarely do). The results vindicated her decision. This illustrates an important aspect of decision making. It is more than cerebral. It involves passion born of deep commitment to the family business, an alignment with its values, analysis of the data, and confidence in one's instincts and abilities. Informed decisions are not perfect decisions, but every decision made, right or wrong, brings more clarity to the path forward. Differentiated leaders can more realistically and quickly assess those decisions. A leader never has crystal clarity, and must learn to deal with a certain amount of ambiguity in any situation without becoming mired in indecision or a desire to placate everyone involved. The future is not set; leaders shape it with decisive action. And their people follow, just as Jean's plant manager did: "You just tell us what we have to do, boss, and we'll do it."

A Sense of Where You Are

On May 30, 2009, Air France Flight 447 pancaked into the equatorial Atlantic Ocean. The airplane turned 225 degrees off course and was flying due west with its nose up, wings nearly level. Thoroughly stalled, it was progressing at merely 107 knots, with a descent rate, despite full thrust, of 11,000 feet per minute. The impact was shattering, and all 228 people on board died instantly. A series of small errors, triggered by a relatively benign malfunction in a speed indicator, turned a state-of-the-art cockpit into a death trap. For an agonizing 4 minutes and 20 seconds preceding the moment of impact, the pilots misinterpreted data streaming at them from the instrument panel. They did precisely the opposite of what their instruments told them to do. The pilots had lost all orientation.[13]

The tragedy was compounded by the fact that everything was behaving exactly as it should. Except for the pilots. They had conceded their skills to automation. Aviation experts tell us that once pilots are put on automation, their manual abilities degrade and their flight-path awareness is dulled. This process is known as deskilling, and in extreme cases, pilots lose all orientation and control. The only way to reverse this process is to turn off autopilot and let the pilots learn to fly again, to "reskill."

It's also known as the OODA loop, a theory developed by fighter pilot John Boyd. OODA stands for observe, orient, decide, and act. Boyd was dubbed "40-second Boyd" for his standing bet that beginning from a position of disadvantage, he could beat any opposing pilot in air combat, maneuvering in less than 40 seconds. No one ever took up Boyd on the bet. He continually outdueled pilots who flew technologically superior planes.[14] Because he abided by the OODA process, he was able to observe changes in the environment, orient himself to the changes, and move to decision and action faster than

---

[13]William Langewiesche, "*Anatomy of an Airline Crash,*" Vanity Fair 650 (October 2014) http://www.airwaypioneers.com.

[14]R. Coram, *Boyd: The Fighter Pilot Who Changed the Art of War* (New York: Back Bay Books, 2002).

his competition. He simply processed information faster. This is the skill of the generative successor.

The acquisition of this skill requires a regular environment, opportunity to practice, and feedback about the accuracy of thoughts and actions. As this skill fully develops, a leader is able to better make in-the-moment intuitive judgments. If a successor is mired in the myth or overcome with his or her own emotions, it slows down this process. A marker of skilled performance is the ability to deal with vast amounts of information swiftly and efficiently. "If it's right, you go faster." John Tyson follows the same principles in chicken production as John Boyd did in aerial combat, and with the same results: He beats his slower competitors. "You make a decision that gives you a competitive advantage; now let's go run with it as fast as [you] can to separate yourself from the competitor."

Reorientation

Lansing Crane took over a company that was oriented more to the past than to the present, more to its history than its future. Technology was passing by Crane & Co., and would render it a relic if it remained stuck in the past. This is called *orientation lock*.[15] It's not that they didn't know what was happening; the data clearly showed their main business deteriorating. But they couldn't interpret what the data were telling them. The reason they got into trouble was the reason they couldn't get out of it. The feedback was getting swallowed by the shadow of their history, prestige, and nostalgia for the way things always were.

Companies tend to do what they know how to do. When they encounter orientation lock, they do what they've always done—even if it doesn't work anymore. Yet reputation and pedigree don't count for much if a company can't deliver and meet current demand.

What the company collectively could not do, Lansing did. He changed himself first, differentiated, and reoriented himself to the company by sitting on its board for several years. Then he struck, quickly and decisively, to change the company. Reoriented, the family business became a global leader in currency security. As Lansing proved himself to be, differentiated leaders are change agents.

---

[15]C. Richards, *Certain to Win: The Strategies of John Boyd Applied to Business* (Xlibris Corporation, 2004).

The Orientation-Locked Family

Families seek to create a sense of stability. This stability is the foundation that nurtures children and gives them a platform to meet the challenges of each life cycle. In order that all needs of all family members are met, as they grow through the life cycles, the family must adapt. Gradually, grandparents, parents, and aunts and uncles must begin to see their children as emerging adults. They must shift their orientation.

Families get orientation lock when they ignore the changes that are happening in the environment (e.g., their kids getting older) and behavior (e.g., their kids becoming more responsible), all of which run counter to the image or orientation that they seek to protect. Husbands and wives, for instance, create family orientation lock when they don't disagree; they get locked into believing a perfect marriage is a conflict-free marriage. Or orientation lock manifests in the family that pretends their father doesn't have an alcohol problem. Or in the family that pretends that a brother, sister, or cousin isn't performing poorly. Orientation lock in a family business is not only a result of a leader rejecting the data that screams "Do things differently!" It also results when a leader protects it at all costs—even when it harms the family legacy. Families that focus on protecting the business or the image of the family at all costs choose protecting image over confronting reality. This creates orientation lock.

A unified family business allows family members to enter and exit the business. Sometimes a leader must make the tough decision to fire the employee when the family vision and mission are at stake. Often, family members flourish outside of the family business, launching their own businesses, for instance, as Jean Moran's brother did when he parted from LMI Packaging. Flowering of a business sometimes happens when family members are allowed to bloom away from their roots. To love is not to possess but to release.

When family business leaders release family members from the business, it does not mean that they place the business over their siblings. Often, the relationship is released to flourish when leaders have the courage and conviction to set their siblings free from something that is not working for them. Take care of the family, and you will keep the business. Neglect the family and you might lose both.

A Decisive Workforce

When "you push responsibility down," says Massimo Ferragamo, "you bring profitability up." A differentiated successor knows how to share and amplify the decision-making process.

Good decisions demonstrate the strength it takes to serve a strong family business over a strong ego. Differentiated leaders make decisions for the good of the family business and take pride in engaging the employees and stakeholders in the decision-making process.

An effective family business energizes and empowers its workforce, its community, and its customers. The authority extends to everybody, as long as they listen to the top-down decisions and know their decisions are traveling up to key decision makers. In this way, the entire organization makes decisions together, with the smaller decisions reflecting the bigger ones.

The most successful leaders create a culture of good decision making, where employees are encouraged and empowered to make suggestions that influence the bigger decisions. Employees who are given genuine decision-making authority can radically increase how much energy and focus they bring to their jobs. The organizational habits and patterns that emerge from employees' independent decisions influence the larger decisions that a leader must make.

The family business has a trust that a nonfamily system doesn't have. This means the leader doesn't need to legislate through bureaucracy. Successors must make it clear to everybody what the end goal is and then let others decide and act. The most successful leaders create a culture of decision making in which employees can make decisions that don't all have to cross the CEO's desk. Quick decision making goes down to the people on the front lines who have immediate access to the data. This is yet another way to protect the organization from orientation lock.

A differentiated leader grasps the implications of decisions that set a long-term course of direction. Input and buy-in from family members, employees, stakeholders, sometimes the customer, and the community are needed. This creates unity around a common goal (the vision). Undifferentiated leaders may fear input because they feel threatened by disagreement or too overconfident in their judgment. Or they may feel so worried about failure that they seek everyone's input. Undifferentiated leaders who seek to please everyone tend to become paralyzed. They realize that it is impossible to make a decision that pleases everyone. In an attempt to maintain their like-ability, they do nothing. Seeking the wrong kind of input also slows down a leader in times when a situation demands decisiveness, such as in a crisis.

Willing to Fail

When he was in high school, Joe Perrino was one of the most competitive athletes in his age bracket in Chicago. "I always wanted to beat the best athlete," he says. But that triumph always eluded him. "I'd go back again and again to try to beat him," Joe says. The easy solution was, "Just don't play him. Play somebody else so you'll feel better about yourself." But Joe was relentless.

"I failed, but I didn't give up. I kept going back. I wouldn't back down."

This life philosophy, now tempered by restraint, has sustained Joe through battles on the front lines of Chicago's most competitive food industry—pizza. "One restaurant failed after we gave it our best effort. I figured out what we did wrong, and how to move ahead. I don't give up." Today, Home Run Inn sells more frozen pizza in the city of Chicago than any other pizza business. "My dad wanted just the one pizza restaurant, and a house attached that he would live and die in," says Joe. Where Nick Perrino saw red lights, his son saw green. Much of life is how you see it. Selling the most pizza is just another green light for Joe, who sees his success extending well beyond him. At 51, Joe had open-heart surgery. He had run into his toughest opponent, his own mortality.

"I will try to beat it, but the odds are, I won't, so I have to prepare for the next generation faster than I expected. I have to start building a stronger family organization. And I have to get out of the way. By the time I'm 60, I'm going to try to be out completely. I'll try to evolve into something else."

Differentiated leaders seem to accept their own mortality. Their decisions construct businesses that will outlast them. Their final decision is knowing when to step down—or to evolve into something else—so that their businesses can continue to thrive into the next generation without them.

10

The Inner Light

A plan to illuminate a successor's path

Greg Bush was grounded.

He had been flying A-10 fighter jets for the United States Air Force for seven years out of the Academy when his father, Jack Bush, recruited him to work in the family business, Linwood Mining and Minerals Corporation, one of the largest limestone mining operations in the United States. The transition from sky to underground was a challenge. Greg wasn't used to slowing down from Mach speed. *Can I be self-actualized doing this after the nonstop adrenaline rush?*

The question immediately made him think of Moose.

Moose was Greg's boss in the Air Force. He told Greg that he would be courted by all sorts of people in the Air Force. "When they come at you," Moose said, "tell them one thing: 'Moose says I'm here to fly jets.'" Following his boss's advice, Greg concentrated on being great at his job and subsequently became the youngest instructor pilot, and one of the youngest evaluation pilots, in England: "I did what Moose told me to do, focused on flying, and considered anything else a distraction."

Moose's good advice then was good advice later when Greg entered the family business. What helped Greg learn to fly helped him learn the mining business. Greg says his plan was simple: "I looked for the place with the biggest problems and learned the system." He figured out what was wrong and how to make it right. He dug in as deeply as he could for the first two and a half years. He followed the rock out of the mine, through the processing plant, asking questions, and learning. Everything else on the conventional management track—Junior Achievement, Rotary Club—was a distraction. He remained singularly focused on the actual work of mining. "Moose gave me the best advice I've ever gotten," Greg says. In a short time, Greg had earned the credibility to fulfill his role as vice president of development.

A simple plan, such as Greg's plan to stay focused, prioritizes a person's life. Stay focused on one vital task and everything else will come. When a leader follows a plan, the family business follows the leader. The business thrives when its leader, having gone through the differentiation process, knows who he is and where he is headed. It's then he can set a due north course for his family and family business. A plan brings a vision down to earth, making it practical and doable. It provides a framework and an agenda that grounds a leader in his values and points him toward his mission—the opportunities to make a difference in the lives of family members, employees, and the community.

Some of the successors in this book developed their plans intuitively, others developed their own planning process, and others tapped into outside resources to guide them in developing their path forward. But the key for each was becoming clear about his or her personal values, mission, and vision and finding alignment with the values, mission, and vision of the family.

The Need for a Personal Strategic Plan

A plan is important for any endeavor, but for the successor of a family business it is critical. In the prologue of this book, I alluded to Bill Wrigley and his strategic plan: to break free of his father's influence, find out who he was as well as what he wanted, and to push the Wrigley Company to reinvent itself. Getting clear about the corporate strategic plan starts with being clear about one's personal strategy. Being clear about one's personal values, mission, and vision lays a foundation for the successor to engage the management team in creating a vision and strategy for the company that aligns with the values and vision of the family.

Bill came to a critical juncture where he was forced to ask himself a simple question, "What's important to me?"

"After I had stopped answering that question based on what my family thought was important for me," Bill laughs, "I finally got honest with myself. I spent a lot of time looking inside to figure it out." That seminal question led him to develop a strategic plan to guide him in his life and his work. Bill regularly updates it to this day. "It keeps me grounded and functions as a kind of map to keep me on course. When I first wrote my plan, ideas suddenly jumped out at me. I surprised myself… 'Wow, that's what I've been looking for. I will introduce it to the company.'" Bill discovered that when he put ideas down on paper, he became more purposeful, and his goals more attainable. His plan helped him cast a vision that he transferred to the company. It was the foundation that enabled him to authentically engage the management team to develop a new corporate strategy for Wrigley, making it better than it was under his father. His father said, "If it ain't broke, don't fix it." For Bill Wrigley Jr., the system was not completely broken, he just wanted to find a better way, more authentic to who he was as a leader.

A personal strategic plan forces answers to the two questions a successor must ask: "What do I want to do with my life?" and "What role do I want to play in our family legacy?" This legacy creates an enormous challenge for the generative family leader: "How do I leverage the legacy for good, rather than getting caught in its shadow? How do I resist becoming an icon? How do I build on the foundation to forward the business to the next generation so they can continue to contribute to the legacy?"

It is a burden of responsibility that requires a strong sense of self. The adjectives—personal and strategic—are important. The plan is personal; it is not a parent's plan, nor is it a family plan, so it may or may not align with the family's plan. The successor has to own it. It's a full expression of who he is and what he wants distinct from the family business and its founder. But it's also strategic. It must leverage the strengths as an individual and the strengths of the family business (its values and mission that have spanned the generations), stewarding the best of the past for the benefit of the future. It serves as a leader's inner compass, so he can ask the right questions for the business: Why are we doing this, and what difference are we making in people's lives? Why does what we do matter to people? These questions reveal the organizational DNA, those qualities that have shaped the organization for decades. The personal strategic plan keeps both the successor and the family business true to the legacy, rather than true to an icon.

This goes a long way toward protecting the successor from creating a cult of personality, which disables next-generation leaders.

A leader whose identity is tied up in the power of the position often creates a cult of personality to bolster a sagging self-esteem. They lead for the adoration and accolades of others. A differentiated leader stays true to plan regardless of public approval. Yes, these leaders are successful, but they are also comfortable with failure. They are transparent when a plan fails; they persevere when they face resistance; and they realize leadership sometimes means being unpopular. These leaders feel good because they stick to plan, not because of what people say about them. Staying in this reality ensures that a new mythology is not created that redoubles a shadow for the next generation of leadership.

A Plan to Differentiate

Jack Bush gave his son the title vice president of development, even though Greg hadn't earned the title. It was Greg's plan, however, to work into the title so the miners wouldn't snicker when he walked into the plant. The challenge for the sons and daughters in a family business is to separate from an established founder so that they command their own destiny and the respect of their family members and employees. But successors must also leverage the strengths of the family business and its legacy, and strengthen it for future generations. To be a favored son and a favorite boss in the family business is a balance that only differentiated leaders can maintain.

Differentiation is critical but challenging for family business leaders. Most children leave their families to go through the differentiation process; their families don't follow them into their working world. The two stay separate so that the child can become a responsible adult, accountable to people who have no vested interest.

For many successors who jump into the family business (and soon face uncertainty about their role), the default is to stick it out and do what the parents want. Relationships entangle the differentiation process. When going straight into a family business, a successor can't make a clean break. He or she remains (and is scrutinized) within a family fishbowl. It makes the differentiation process that much harder. It's difficult, though not impossible, to contribute authentically when the successor is unclear about who she is and the impact she wants to have on the world (broadly) and the family business (generally).

A differentiated and generative leader opens him- or herself up to enormous opportunity and reward: stewardship of the family legacy for the next generation. It's why Wrigley Jr. didn't run away from Wrigley Sr.; it's why Greg Bush stopped flying and started digging; and it's why Lansing Crane left a prestigious private practice to revive the family business. Building a family legacy sustained across generations is as rewarding (if not more rewarding) than pursuing fame or riches on one's own. But it has a more enduring impact on the life of the family, employees, and community. In a family business especially, nothing is more important than building relationships with the people who matter to the family business—the family stakeholders, employees, and community. A family business generates and sustains these relationships across generations.

Differentiation is the pathway to this generative leadership. And a personal strategic plan is the best way to engage the process. It forces a leader to get clear about who he is and what he wants. This is particularly important when the family wants a leader to do only what it wants, or when it doesn't want the new leader at all. Differentiation's two extremes are fusion and disengagement. The fused family is so emotionally entangled that an individual fears to assert his or her identity because it might lead to family strife. The family views it simply: To be different is to invite conflict, and conflict is essential to differentiate. A fused family will thus fight the leader attempting to differentiate. Disengaged families, on the other hand, are so detached from one another that they lack a common bond. Healthy family businesses rest on a point between the two poles of fusion and disengagement. A differentiated successor provides just enough friction to ignite a family business that has gone cold, enough oxygen to keep the fire burning, and the boundaries to keep it from blazing out of control.

When Greg Bush came back to the family business, he had established a strong sense of who he was. "I got out of town," he says. "I was gone long enough and far enough away, and my life was different enough that I felt very comfortable making my own decisions. And live my life for me."

As an example, Greg grew a goatee, an emblem of independence. "Take that thing off," his brother said. "Mom doesn't like it."

"But I like it," I told him. "It's good for mom to have little treat now and then, to give her a little spark."

Growing a goatee is symbolic of what all successors must do. Be authentic. It's not an easy task for a successor to resist family expectations and stay true to his calling. For Greg Bush, his ultimate calling was CEO. For another, it might be a different position. Over almost 20 years of teaching successors in our Next Generation Leadership Institute and Family Business Stewardship Institute, we have had individuals who thought they wanted to be CEO, but after doing some real reflection, felt that they wanted to pursue other things in their life. One chose to become the VP of HR, another chose to leave and join the army, and another chose to leave the family business and start her own company separate from the family business. Not every successor should be CEO of a company, and not every family can breed CEOs of multimillion-dollar and billion-dollar companies. The question a successor must ask is, "What's the right place for me in terms of what I want, what I am good at, and the sacrifices I want to make?" A differentiated leader will not try to be another legend, but will remain steadfast to both his vision for his life and the family business and its legacy.

Successors bring to bear the best of who they are and what they do to bring out the best in the family business and the people in their employ. When they know who they are and where they are going, they find the right place for others. Leaders follow an inner calling, and people follow them. Creating and following a strategic plan makes this possible.

True North

A strategic plan is the blueprint of its architect, the differentiated leader who wants to continue to build the family business. It shapes his choices, tells him what's important, and reminds him who he is, what he's doing, and why he's doing it. A strategic plan keeps leaders pointed true north. It corrects them when they head off course.

In short, it holds a leader accountable.

The adage, "Measure twice, cut once," applies to more than carpentry. Leaders tend to be doers, and all leaders at some point succumb to the tyranny of the urgent, the myriad of things that must be done *now*. The problem is, there are always things, and it's always *now*. It's hard to resist the relentless call to do and instead stop yourself, step away, take a breath, and think about what you're doing and why you're doing it. This takes time, attention, and considerable mental effort. Successors must regularly set aside that time to reflect and evaluate, at least twice a year, perhaps more in the beginning when a new leader has to do more heavy lifting. A strategic plan can increase leaders' accountability to achieving their vision.

Accountability starts with writing down the plan. Floating ideas tend to disappear; putting them to paper creates an orientation that will help the successor make decisions about where to spend resources (time, money, energy). Read the plan to yourself and to the people most important to you. For true accountability, a strategic plan must separate the merely interesting ideas from the crucial. It must include the essentials of values, mission, vision, and an action plan. This takes time; it is a process of gaining clarity. Bill Wrigley did not wake up one morning and say, "I am going to write a strategic plan today." It germinated over hours in airplanes to dozens of business trips around the world, as he clarified what it was that he wanted, what it meant for the company, and most of all, what it meant for his relationship with Bill Sr.

Bill Jr. struck a balance between fusion—running the company just like his father—and disengagement, leaving the business completely (an option he seriously considered before his father got sick). Bill Wrigley's strategic plan helped him identify his purpose, distilled to 10 words that I've repeated throughout this book: "Respect the past, but do what's right for the future."

Values

The heart of Bill's plan that inspired his innovative philosophy of leadership was in his practical values: Don't try to do too much. Don't isolate. Educate yourself. Entertain multiple points of view and influence. Anticipate pushback but don't be pushy; respect the family values. And be a problem solver.

Values are the genetic sequence of a leader's soul, and the strategic plan maps its genetic code. The work of self-reflection over months and even years maps personal values distinct from parents' values. A successor is not a clone of the founder. This is vital, not only because it shows a leader who he is but because it brings a successor's

DNA into the mix, so that the company is strengthened. Strong genes get stronger when they are diversified. Massimo Ferragamo describes this type of DNA:

> It's what you cannot touch anywhere, but it's there and it's holding all the company together … if you change a company's DNA, it becomes another company. It often fails because people are trying to make stuff that isn't true to the name and the brand. So you have to respect the DNA, and allow it to evolve. What it is today is the same but also different from five years ago. It's genetic adaptation. Leaders who know what it was can also interpret what it will be.

Values are the foundation of the plan. They are clarified over time, but they don't change. Jean Moran identified her three values—full-expression, self-awareness, leadership—as they emerged from the tests she faced, mistakes she made, and tears she wept. "My values got me through," Jean says, "and I've worked with a lot of leadership coaches and done a lot of work on myself to identify them."

"Values are what help companies walk the walk." When Bill Wrigley became CEO, he reinforced the values that had helped Wrigley Corporation "walk the walk": trust, dignity, respect. He realigned the company to its historic true north, and strengthened it with his personal core values, which were different from his father's: listening, empowering people, and trusting them to make decisions that would help reinvigorate the company. Pierre Taittinger's aligned his values with the two-century-old tradition of the Champagne Way.

Mission

The mission gives the values a target. It answers the question, "What impact do I want to have?"

The military gave Greg Bush a very specific understanding of taking on and accomplishing a mission. "The military does not pay well, and it's largely made up of kids who love to party. But come Monday morning, they are there for one reason, to accomplish the mission, whatever it is, to defend their country." The loyalties that form around that mission are fierce. A soldier fights for his country, while sacrificing his life for his brother-in-arms.

Greg struggled for a year and a half trying to redefine a sense of mission, for himself first, and then for the family business. Jack Bush gave his son a title but not a mission; Greg had to discover his own mission as he spent time with the employees, working alongside them, asking questions, listening, and finding out that for many employees, working for Linwood was nothing more than a job." Greg realized that he needed to translate a paycheck into a sense of purpose. Greg Bush says of his mission:

> We have three generations of families who have worked for us, and for whom we are responsible. 700 families with three or four people per family is a lot of people who are counting on us. We need to protect them by doing our job well, make good decisions to ensure the strength and stability of this company. And prepare it for the next generation of leadership. That's my mission. And I am bringing everyone along with me.

Greg Bush reflects the best of family business leadership. He learned to harness the power of the family business values while providing clarity of vision and a mission that benefits generations to come. Not every family business has that ability to develop the long-term view. But if families can support the development of the next generation in the right way, the next generation is equipped to step into leadership with a clearer sense that the business is about more than just them.

Action Plan

"When you don't know where you are going, any path will get you there" is a popular adage that pertains to family business succession. A successor must choose his or her unique path. Leaders who have clearly articulated their values, vision, and mission do not wander, or pick the easiest path in front of them. They often take the road less traveled, and that makes all the difference. These leaders have clarity of purpose. Purpose compels them to act because it brings into focus the things that matter the most. When a leader acts in line with his purpose, he creates a way forward. Greg Bush had a mission to serve and protect all the families in the employ of McCarthy-Bush Corporation, but his action plan started with one step, one task: take on one problem area, find out what it revealed, and bear down on it until he learned everything there was to know about the process.

He followed through until he understood all the processes, and the company prospered under his leadership.

When Bill Wrigley became chief executive of the The Wrigley Company at the age of 37, he granted a rare interview with *Forbes* magazine in which he said, "I see my role as taking a late nineteenth-century company and bringing it into the twenty-first century with guns blazing."[1] He walked the walk and stayed with it. In two years, the company bought back millions of shares, created a health division, and bought part of a gum technology company. "Almost everything they said they were going to do a year ago, they've executed on," Mr. Katzman at Deutsche Banc said. "That's rare."[2] That's following a strategic plan.

A Flexible Plan

A few years ago, I took my own advice and developed a strategic plan for my business. I got clear about what I do and stand for: Building healthy families and healthy businesses. What I do in both my personal and professional life I try to gear toward these two goals. Am I perfect at doing this? Absolutely not. I get caught up in life and get excited by ideas. But a strategic plan helps me to manage the distractions. To create a layer of accountability, I have shared these goals with close friends and colleagues who I can turn to for accountability and feedback.

A plan, however, is never so rigid that it can't be reshaped. As my worldview shifts, my strategic plan will follow suit. Generally, a mission is constant, and the vision and goals, as outlined in a strategic plan, adjust based on circumstances. This is a trait of a successful leader: agility. Leaders with focus can read the feedback and adjust course when circumstances change.

It is akin to being a pilot and filing a flight plan. You create a plan for how you are going to get from point A to point B, but once you get up in the air, you might encounter turbulence, storms, and wind that make you adjust your plan. Sometimes you must land in a different place.

---

[1]David Barbosa, "A Young Heir Has New Plans at Old Company; Bill Wrigley Is Aggressive in Meeting Rivals Head-On," *New York Times* (August 28, 2001).

[2]Ibid.

Let There Be Love

A strategic plan is sometimes a high-wire tightrope. The strongest leaders have the balance to stay on and walk to the other side when even their most loyal supporters resist them. "I've never gotten much pushback from nonfamily," says Greg Bush. "It's mostly been family."

Greg walked this tightrope when the McCarthy-Bush board elected Greg as CEO to replace his father, after it became clear that his older brother Larry's talents would be better suited to the role of CFO. Like his brother, Larry had launched his own career before stepping into the family business. Greg assumed Larry would seize the reins of leadership—and do it better. But the challenge in any succession process is matching each successor's skill sets to a job where they can add value.

"This is going to disrupt the family," Greg told Larry. In fact, it created competition between Greg and his other brother, Joe. Following his simple plan to learn, stay focused, and do a good job, Greg earned the respect and trust of the Linwood employees and the executive board of the McCarthy-Bush Corporation. His followers had already granted him the authority to lead. And now they wanted to make it official.

"I pretty much knew going in that it was going to be that way. I felt like I was the most qualified for the position, because I had best prepared for it."

"But the fallout was as bad as you can imagine," Greg says, "with the perception among some family members that I had gamed the system." His Dad had not managed the family expectations; they expected a vote but got a decree of the board. Greg was the new CEO of McCarthy-Bush, and for five years he and Joe were somewhat alienated.

Greg credits his ability to remain emotionally objective, a critical quality for a family business leader who must navigate the thin line between keeping the family peace and doing what's best for the business. "I have an ability to lay aside the family issues," he says, "and all the excess emotional baggage, and look at problems logically."

When a family leader makes a true north decision that conflicts with the family, he will also need the strength to hold on and seek to rebuild family relationships through the emotional fallout. "If you're in any contest at all where you can win or lose," said the great director

Mike Nichols, "try to win." For Greg Bush, who prefers winning to losing, following his true north ultimately was a win-win, but it also had a cost. Greg and Joe have repaired the relationship, and Greg feels that Joe would concede, that his skills are better aligned with the role that he has today.

"But our relationship changed," says Greg. "I'm not just one of the Bush boys. I'm different, and that's forever. But I felt I had to be true to me, and that's my rock."

Family businesses, even the best ones, are not Camelot. "That was my dad's vision for the business," says Greg. He thought it would be the "perfect opportunity for every family member. Everybody comes in and nobody ever leaves. The business cradles all of us."

Greg has a less romantic version. "A family business allows you to be yourself. But it comes with a lot of family conflict, and it's never completely resolved. That's heaven, but it's not family."

The family business gives family members wonderful options and opportunities to be and do their best. And that's different for everybody.

"I have a brother who works for us, but his passion is coaching wrestling." Greg says. "He loves it. Shouldn't the family business provide him the opportunity to coach wrestling and do what he loves? That's my vision for the family business. It gives each of us an opportunity to live the life we love. What a great thing."

Let There Be Light

Like many Italian sons, Massimo Ferragamo is strongly attached to his mother. But he is no mama's boy. "When the patriarch or matriarch is too strong," Massimo says, "no flowers blossom under the shadow of an oak tree. My mother was as solid as an oak tree, but she let the light in. She never did anything that impeded the growth of her sons and daughters. She had an incredible value for people, and would let them do what they were supposed to do. Once you develop trust, let the person work."

Wanda Ferragamo established inviolable principles and values in her children, and a sense of trust in each other and in themselves.

"All a child needs is two or three principles that will anchor them through their lives," Massimo says. "And then give them room to grow, so that their personality can come out." All six Ferragamo children have expressed their personalities through an ever-expanding business that includes clothing, handbags, accessories, hotels, and wineries. Enlightened parents ground their children in principles, and then release them to become their own people. Children of strong founders do not become leaders without that inner light.

The light within always shines outward. Family businesses with enlightened leadership illuminate the way for community and society, providing opportunity for those outside the family circle to live a life they love. When parents can support the development of the next generation in the right way, the next generation can step into leadership guided by the inner light of values, mission, and vision—and then shine that light outward. It's the very thing that allows the next-generation leader to step out of the darkness of the founder's shadow.

Generational family businesses have the opportunity to do amazing things that other businesses can't. Wanda Ferragamo remains at her clan's center, the torchbearer for her husband's guiding light, and the children have built a global empire from their father's creative fire and seminal thought, "Beauty has no limits."

Joe Perrino of Home Run Inn has close to a 30 percent market share in the Chicago area in the frozen pizza industry in the most competitive market in the country. Home Run Inn's closest competitor, Nestlé, has 11 percent.

Mike Hamra's Dream Manager program helps his employees live their dreams. After hiring Christie Reed as his Dream Manager, Mike first tested the concept on himself. Working with Christie, Mike, who already had his pilot's license, developed and achieved his dream plan to fly a large jet. Through Mike's Dream Manager program, a "Dream Culture" has emerged. It has inspired them to create HERO (Hamra Employees Reaching Out), a program that has raised over $600,000 to support their fellow Hamra employees, giving over $200,000 in grants to support 235 employees.

Family-owned businesses don't just build the economy, they build communities. They are the stitching in the fabric of our towns, our cities, and nations.

Epilogue: Stepping out of the Shadows and into the Light of Your Leadership

The succession stories that we have heard throughout this book show us that it is possible to follow in the footsteps of great leaders and develop a leadership style that is true to who you are. I'd like to tell you that there is an easy five-step process to stepping out of the shadows, but the process is not linear, it is iterative. What is important is to build a consistent practice at examining your growth and development as a leader, getting feedback, and being clear about your values, your mission, and your vision for your life. There are as many paths out of the shadows as there are successors. There are executive education style programs like the Next Generation Leadership Institute at Loyola, Next Gen communities like the community at the Family Business Network North America, and great opportunities to learn through YPO, Vistage, and local family business centers. But, I'd like to leave you with one possible framework, with questions to help you identify the most powerful myths at work in your family and business, as well as understand what they mean for you and the challenges that you face. Some of these questions can help lead you to an action plan toward achieving your vision for your life.

Identifying the Myths

Often, when we feel most stuck in our growth and development in a family business, it is the power of the myths and stories that we tell as a family about our parents, about our families, about our businesses, and about ourselves as successors that keeps us stuck. Identifying and understanding the myths that are most powerful is critical to helping get us unstuck and out of the shadows. The following questions can help you in identifying and understanding the myths at play in your family and business:

- Who are the individuals who are most talked about in your family?
- What are the stories that people tell about them?
- Are these stories supportive of your growth and development, or do they make it more difficult?
- What are the stories that people tell about your family and your business?
- Are these stories supportive of your growth and development, or do they make it more difficult?
- What impact have these stories had on you?
- What impact have these stories had on the family?
- What impact have these stories had on the business?

Self

Getting clear about who you are, what you believe, and what you want for your life will help you communicate more clearly with your family, and increase the likelihood of finding a meaningful path toward a generative leadership role in your family and business. This starts with your mission, vision, and values.

- **Mission**—What is my reason for being?
  1. What impact do I want to have in the world?
  2. What am I trying to accomplish in my personal and professional lives?
- **Values**—What are the principles and values that are most important to me that I want to use to guide my behaviors? What are my fundamental beliefs?
  1. What are the five values that are most important to me in my life?
  2. What values most represent who I am?
  3. What do my behaviors say about my values?
  4. What impact do I want to have in the world? On my relationships? On my family business?
- **Vision**—What do I want my life to look like one, three, or five years from now? In my personal life, my professional life, and my life in the community? How will my values support me in achieving this vision?

How do my mission/vision/values relate to that of my spouse/family? Are they aligned? Where do they conflict?

1. What knowledge or skill sets are critical toward achieving my vision?
2. Do I have these skill sets, or do I need to develop them?
3. What will it look like if I achieve this vision? What will success look like? How will I measure it?

What is my vision for how I want to show up in the important relationships in my life?

What is my vision for the role that I want to play in my family business?

a. Family member (father, mother, sibling, cousin …)
b. Supportive shareholder
c. Engaged shareholder
d. Family leader
e. Board member
f. Board chair
g. Employee
h. Senior leadership in the company

What is my vision for the role that I want to play in my community?

a. Philanthropic leader
b. Civic leader

What is my vision for what I want to do for work?

a. What am I good at?
b. When am I happiest?
c. What am I passionate about?
d. Where will my gifts be best utilized? (family business, elsewhere?)

What work is aligned with my skills?

What type of environment or culture aligns with my values?

What type of lifestyle do I want to lead?

Building Internal Credibility

1. Personality assessment tools
   i. DISC
   ii. Myers-Briggs
   iii. Strength Finders

    iv. Big Five

    v. Hogan Assessment

2. 360 instruments

    i. Leadership Versatility index – Kaplan Devries

    ii. 360 By Design – Center for Creative Leadership

    iii. Voices 360 – Lominger

3. Key questions

    i. Where have I had the most success in my life?

    ii. What do others tell me that I am good at?

    iii. What skills were necessary to achieve that success?

    iv. What activities make me feel the most engaged?

    v. What are my greatest strengths?

    vi. What are my greatest weaknesses?

4. Dealing with failure

    i. Where have I failed?

    ii. Why did I fail?

    iii. What can I learn from this failure?

    iv. How will this help/hurt the pursuit of my vision?

5. Being accountable to yourself: Ideal Versus Actual Self

    i. Do I live the values that I have identified?

    ii. Do I deliver on what I say I am going to do?

    iii. Would others say the same about me?

    iv. Where are the gaps?

    v. What actions can I take in order to fill the gaps?

6. Where can I get the following?

    i. Feedback

    ii. Advice

    iii. Support

Building External Credibility

Skills

1. What knowledge will I need in order to be credible in my leadership role? or to achieve my vision?
2. What skills will I need in order to be successful in my role? To achieve my vision?
3. How can I gain this knowledge and these skill sets?

Reputation

1. What reputation do I want to have?
2. Do my actions and does my performance align with that reputation?
3. Where are the gaps?

Roles

1. What is my current role (or roles)?
2. What is great about this role (these roles)?
3. What would I change?
4. How do the roles that I currently play in my family business and community align with my mission, vision, and values?

Anticipating Change

1. What are the changes that will occur in my life in the next one, three, or five years?
2. What are the implications of these changes for achieving my vision?

Relationships

1. What are the most important relationships in my life?
2. What is the status of those relationships?
3. What do I want those relationships to look like?

A

Research Note

The goal of this book was to help readers to understand the experience of a successor, from the successor's point of view. After almost 20 years of hearing the stories of successors in our Next Generation Leadership Institute, I had some ideas about the challenges that faced successors, but I wanted to know more. I wanted to understand, from the successor's point of view, what it was like to take the reins of a storied family business, and I wanted to be able to share that knowledge with others who might benefit from their stories.

To take this challenge on, I used grounded research theory, a methodology pioneered by Barney Glaser and Anselm Strauss. Under the guidance and tutelage of Dr. Torsten Pieper at Kennesaw State University, and with the help of Dr. Corinna Lindow and Dr. Isa Botero, we culled through the hundreds and hundreds of pages of interviews, developing codes to denote the themes that were emerging from the interviews.

I interviewed 28 different successors before we reached saturation. The interviewees ranged from second generation to eleventh generation. They were 25 men and 3 women. And their companies ranged from $20 million in sales to multibillion-dollar companies such as Wrigley and Tyson. We coded interviews from these 28 successors, and these interviews generated 1,949 unique codes. Those codes were then grouped and narrowed down into segments in order to find the commonalities across interviews.

These themes or groups form the foundation of this book. Building on these common themes from our successors, I have sought to share their wisdom, and also to inject my experiences in working with successors for almost 20 years on how to deal with the challenges identified therein.

Although the stories and experiences found here are compelling, this grounded research approach really opens the door for future research to explore the themes explored in this book. For instance, it would be greatly beneficial for future research to explore the practice of a successor working outside the business to understand its true impact on the differentiation process. It would be interesting to understand if successors who carry the same first name as their parents encounter a bigger shadow. I think that future research could also develop a larger pool of female successors to explore gender differences in the experiences of successors.

A Generative Retreat: $1/3$ Activity (Body), $1/3$ Reflection (Self), $1/3$ Planning (Future)

One of the biggest challenges of any leader is managing time and priorities. It is important for the generative successor to set aside time for reflection, renewal, and planning. We need to take time out of our days and our lives to reflect and get clear about our priorities as well as to assess how we are progressing in the pursuit of our goals. Many leaders that I talk to make a regular practice of making this time available and renewing their sense of purpose and energy.

My belief is that a retreat such as this should address body, mind, and spirit and at the same time allow for the creation of clear goals and objectives.

Body: Taking care of your body and your health is essential for you to be the best leader that you can be. It is easy with a busy schedule to loose sight of the importance of sleep, exercise, and eating well. These are the foundation that give a leader the energy to lead.

Self: You need to take time to reflect on both who you are and what you value, as well as your mission, vision, and values. Creating the space to do this reflection is critical.

Future: There is an old adage that says, "If you don't know where you are going, any road will get you there." Setting aside time to create clear plans, goals, and objectives to make your vision a reality increases the likelihood that your vision will come true.

Below is one framework for a reflective retreat to get a successor started.

1. Creating a generative mind and body – assess, get clear about, and engage in …
   a. Values
   b. Exercise
   c. Diet
   d. Mindfulness
   e. Spirituality
2. Creating a generative family life
   a. What do I want my family life to look like in one, three, or five years?
   b. What transitions will I go through?
   c. What transitions will my family go through?
   d. How will these transitions affect the achievement of my vision?
   e. What goals and action steps will help me get there?
3. Creating a generative work life
   a. What do I want my work life to look like in one, three, or five years? What transitions will I go through?
   b. What transitions will my family go through?
   c. How will these transitions affect the achievement of my vision?
   d. What goals and action steps will help me get there?
4. Sharing the plan
   a. Who do I need to share my plan with?
   b. Who do I want feedback, advice, and support from?

About the Author

Andrew Keyt is an internationally known business strategist and succession planning expert for family owned businesses. He has established a reputation globally for his exceptional ability to advise large family-owned businesses, resolve family conflict, and restore communication. He is one of the few experts called upon in family emergency transitions to help them discover invisible opportunities and solve seemingly impossible problems.

Keyt is a contributing writer to several industry and national publications, including *Family Business Magazine, Family Business Review,* and *Campden FB.* His acute family business insights have been featured in *The Wall Street Journal, Chicago Tribune, Los Angeles Times, Fortune Magazine, Smart Money, The Economist,* and *Families in Business.*

Keyt is the **Executive Director at the Loyola University Chicago Family Business Center** (www.luc.edu/fbc) dedicated to helping multigenerational family-owned businesses grow, transition, and learn. The center serves some of the largest family firms in the United States and Canada, approximately 100 member family businesses ranging in size from $25 million to $8 billion in annual sales.

As executive director, Keyt advances the center's research efforts, developing initiatives such as the Loyola Guidelines for Family Business Boards, Emergency Management Transition, Family Influences on Strategic Planning, Family Business Board Compensation, Non-Family CEOs and the Family Business, Family Shareholder Buyouts, and the American Family Business Survey. Loyola's Family Business Center received the Family Firm Institute (FFI) international award and was ranked by CNN.Money and Fortune Small Business as one of the top six family business programs.

Keyt is also the CEO and president of FBN North America (www.fbn-na.org), the North American Chapter of the Family Business Network International (FBN-I). FBN-I is a global network of over

3000 family businesses dedicated to the multigenerational success and sustainability of family firms. FBN is the premier global organization serving family firms.

Keyt is also President and Founder of Keyt Consulting (www .andrewkeyt.com), a private firm that assists family enterprises with succession, family, and business strategic planning, family conflict and communication by working with adult sibling/cousin teams, and next generation leadership development. Having been a member of his own family partnership and having served as manager in two family-owned firms, Keyt has firsthand experience with family business challenges.

Keyt is an acclaimed keynote speaker on family business topics at conferences all around the world including Campden Publishing Families Business Conferences, Family Business Network International Conferences (Colombia, Finland, India, Ireland, Singapore, United Kingdom, United States), United States Association of Small Business & Entrepreneurship, FBE Conference, University of Jyvaskyla in Finland, Association of Mergers & Acquisitions Advisors Conference, Association of Fundraising Professionals, Independent Grocers Association, University of Alberta-Canada, Cornell University, Crain's Chicago Small Business Forum, Presidents Forum Retreat, ABA National Trust School, Shoe Retailers Association, The Northern Trust Corporation, World President's Organization, Harris Bank, and Capital Bank & Trust.

Keyt holds a master's degree in family systems theory from Northwestern University with a concentration in family business and an MBA in Family Business with Honors from Kennesaw State University. He is a cum laude graduate of Kenyon College.

Keyt currently serves as a governor on the auxiliary board for the Steppenwolf Theater, a member of the Advocate Illinois Masonic Hospital Charitable Council, and the Advisory Board for the Center for Urban Research & Learning at Loyola University Chicago. He has served on the Alumni Council of Kenyon College and the Board of Deacons of the Fourth Presbyterian Church of Chicago. As a volunteer with the Leukemia Society of America, Keyt has completed six marathons to raise money for leukemia research. An avid singer, Keyt has performed in classical choirs, jazz clubs, and popular settings.

Index

accountability
  of employees, 59, 60, 118
  in family businesses, 127–128
  in government bureaucracy, 59, 60
  through strategic plan, 158, 159, 162
  of successors, 47–48, 50, 56, 69, 143
Air France Flight, 447, 147
Amway, 89–91, 94, 101
Andringa, Mary Vermeer, 4, 28, 125, 142
authenticity
  and blind spots, 47
  cultivating, 45
  of family myth, 5
  of leaders, 43, 44
  and organizational success, 44
  and responsibility, 49
  of successors, 22, 26, 29, 44, 158
authority, assuming, 13
autonomy
  of children, 12
  of employees, 130
awards programs, 131

belief systems, 117
Best Washington Uniform Supply, Inc., 46
blind spots, 46–47, 52
Botero, Isa, 173
Bowen, Murray, 22

Bowen Center for the Study of the Family, 30
Boyd, John, 147, 148
Branson, Richard, 67
Brown, Brene, 9, 45, 144
Burke, John, 50, 53–55, 84, 95
Burke, Richard, 50, 53, 54, 55
Bush, Greg, 153–154, 156, 157–158, 160–161, 163–164
Bush, Jack, 153, 156, 161
Bush, Joe, 163, 164
Bush, Larry, 163
business school, 145

chief executive officers (CEOs)
  compensation to, 126
  as motivators, 130
  vs. other leadership roles, 81, 158
  replacing, 84
  successors as, 94
children. *See also* successors
  accountability of, 47–48, 50
  development of, 23–24, 32, 65
  naming of, 17
  parent-pleasing by, 9–11, 31, 96
  perception of parents, 7–8
  providing challenges for, 68–69, 142
  values learned by, 79
coaching
  and differentiation process, 63
  for family conflicts, 116
  to increase self-awareness, 34

collaboration
  in family problem solving, 116
  as leadership style, 42
  as life skill, 12
  by successors, 113
Collins, Jim, 130
communication
  in family businesses, 104, 168
  among family members, 116–117
  between successor and family,
    168
competition
  effects of, 113–114
  among family members, 163
  gaining advantage over, 148
conflict
  in differentiation, 157
  among family members, 104,
    106, 116, 163–164
  in succession process, 22, 29–30
corporations, employee motivation
  in, 129
Crane, Lansing (Lanse), 94,
  135–142, 148, 157
Crane, Stephen, 135
Crane, Winthrop Murray, 139–140
Crane, Zenas, 135
Crane & Co., 135–137, 138, 139,
  140, 148
credibility
  through accountability, 47–48
  and differentiation, 131
  earning, 26, 62, 92, 93, 134
  external, 43, 48–49, 75, 170–171
  among family members, 105
  internal, 15, 43, 54, 68, 169–170
  loss of, 80, 94
  and parentification, 13
  and self-awareness, 33, 35, 123
  and successor ambition, 51,
    54, 93
  successor development of, 4, 27,
    31, 43, 52, 63

sustaining, 91–93
testing, 106
criticism. See feedback
cult of personality, 76, 94, 98, 122,
  134, 144, 155–156
culture
  of family, 113
  organizational, 9, 79, 83, 94, 117,
    122, 127, 150
  transmitted by myth, 4

Daring Greatly (Brown), 9, 144
decision making
  for company change, 137,
    138–139
  distribution of, 128, 150
  among family members, 106
  honed through action, 62
  by inexperienced successors, 51
  influenced by others, 26
  by leaders, 30, 60–61, 99,
    140–142
  and perfectionism, 143–144
  process of, 145–148
deskilling, 147
devaluation, 14–15
DeVos, Dick (son), 63, 89–91, 94,
  95–96, 97–98, 101, 122, 126,
  142
DeVos, Richard (father), 89, 90, 94,
  95, 98
differentiation
  and accepting responsibility, 122
  and decision making, 138–139,
    140
  and devaluation, 15
  and dysfunctional family
    patterns, 61
  and leadership, 26, 29–30, 92,
    123–124, 131, 134, 140, 151,
    157
  and life cycle, 22–25
  and names of successors, 17

parental humanization in, 28
parental role in, 9, 33
process of, 22, 25, 44, 91, 156
self-awareness in, 33–34, 123
and success, 31, 106
by successors, 9–11, 22, 25–27, 39, 61
via outside work, 63, 71
diversification, 137
dividends, 108–109, 116
Domain Carneros, 85
Drive (Pink), 129–130

egocentrism
and decision making, 150
family mythology based in, 4–5, 117
and self-awareness, 123
vs. shared recognition, 131
vs. sociocentrism, 76
of successors, 27, 124
of tyrants, 26
emotional intelligence
within families, 106
function of, 99–100
of leaders, 49, 69, 124, 163
empathy
within family, 106
in generative leaders, 78
in successors, 30, 49
employees
accountability of, 59, 60, 118, 127–128
family members as, 118–119
input from, 63–64, 150
managing, 58, 121–122
motivation of, 129–130, 132
mythologizing by, 8
programs supporting, 165
recognition of, 130–131
relationship of leaders to, 125–126, 128, 134
responsibility for, 99, 122

self-interested, 127
of small businesses vs. corporations, 129
entitlement, sense of
avoiding, 30, 55–56
creating, 12
vs. success via work, 52–53
in tyrants, 26
and victimization, 15

failure
and idealization, 11, 142–143
as learning experience, 7, 36, 60, 64–68, 97, 144, 151
and parentification, 13
by predecessors, 28
responsibility for, 49–50
and self-esteem, 65, 143, 156
by successors, 50–51
families
building resilience in, 116–117
children separating from, 24
dysfunctional, 61
as launching pads, 69
orientation lock in, 149
parental absence in, 8
protecting image of, 5, 149
family businesses
awards programs in, 131
compensation within, 126
competition within, 113–114, 163
decision making in, 137–151
employees of, 127–128, 132
entitlement in, 55
founder vs. family as focus of, 114–117
idealization in, 12
identity of, 82
leadership of. *See* leaders; successors
mission of. *See* mission
opportunities unique to, 165

family businesses *(continued)*
  organizational pattern of, 117
  relationships within, 94,
    104–105, 140, 149, 157,
    163–164
  reorienting, 148, 149
  success of, 107–110, 137–138
  values in. *See* values
  vision in. *See* vision
Family Business Network North
  America, 167
Family Business Stewardship
  Institute, 158
family legacy
  and dividends, 108–109
  establishing, 54, 94–95
  and family relationships, 105
  financial support for, 116
  founder impact on, 3
  leveraging, 34, 78
  and orientation lock, 149
  and resilience, 117
  and successful leadership, 94–95
  successor contribution to, 39
  successor stewardship of, 7, 16,
    29, 61, 84, 101, 134, 155, 156,
    157
family mythologies
  deconstructing, 27–30
  development of, 7–9
  function of, 47
  ideal vs. reality in, 6–7, 8, 77, 99
  impact on children, 10–11
  interpreting, 16–17, 167–168
  negative effects of, 4–6, 15,
    32–33, 65–66
  positive effects of, 3–4
  and successor differentiation, 31,
    63, 139
Federal Communications Commission (FCC), 58–59
feedback
  in decision making, 145, 148

  and failure, 66
  among family members, 105,
    107, 119
  to generative leaders, 77, 98
  and insecurity, 100
  objective, 48
  responding to, 162
  role of, 69
Ferragamo, Massimo, 1–3, 9–10,
  13, 14, 16–17, 25, 29, 78, 82,
  95, 96, 115, 142, 160, 164
Ferragamo, Salvatore, 1–3, 6, 14,
  16, 95
Ferragamo, Wanda, 3, 14, 115, 164,
  165
Ferragamo USA, 2, 16–17, 25, 165
firing. *See* termination
Fortune 500, 107
founders/predecessors
  and business growth, 9
  commitment to purpose, 79
  control relinquished by, 57, 70
  humanizing, 27–28, 97, 125
  power of, 7, 54, 77, 123, 143–144
  relationship with successors, 22,
    51, 164–165
  self-confidence vs.
    self-absorption in, 95–96
  vision of, 126

Glaser, Barney, 173
Goleman, Daniel, 49
Good to Great (Collins), 130
Great Depression, 2, 4, 6, 25
Grittani, Mary, 19
Grittani, Vincent, 19

Hamra, Mike, 57–60, 63, 69–70, 84,
  99, 132, 133, 165
Hamra, Sam, 57, 60, 69, 70
Hamra Enterprises, 57, 58, 60,
  69–70, 99, 132
Haub, Karl-Erivan, 4, 17, 71

Haubt, Lawrence (pseudonym), 143
Haubt, Mary (pseudonym), 143
Haubt, Peter (pseudonym), 143
Hefner, Christie, 41–44, 45, 54, 127, 134
Hefner, Hugh, 41–44, 134
heroic stories. *See also* family mythologies
    deconstructing, 28–29
    effects of, 2–3, 131
    and perfectionism, 143–144
    rationalization for, 8
HERO (Hamra Employees Reaching Out) program, 165
Hidden Champions (Simon), 108
Hoare, Alexander, 36, 82, 109
Hoare, Bella, 35–37, 38, 62, 63, 109
Hoare & Co., 35, 62, 82, 109–110
Hoffer, Eric, 12
Home Run Inn, 19–21, 31, 39, 66, 81, 151, 165
hothouse parenting, 12
human project, 74

Ideal Industries, 31, 85–87, 116
idealization
    vs. devaluation, 14
    function of, 47
    as hero creation, 28
    negative effects of, 32–33
    of parents, 8, 9, 28
    of successor, 11–13, 45–46, 142–143
ideals, developing, 122
identity
    as adult, 24, 44–45, 47
    crisis of, 26
    and differentiation, 22, 31
    and failure, 66
    of family business, 82
    and idealization, 11, 12, 32
    ideal vs. actual, 43, 52

of predecessors, 70
through self-awareness, 35
of successors, 5, 10, 29, 30, 32–33, 38, 46, 63
values as part of, 79–80
image
    differentiating, 26–27
    of family, 5, 149
infantilization, 13–14
innovation
    by employees, 128
    and failure, 65
    and imitation of past, 78, 141
    as leader motivation, 94
    source of, 144
integrity, 79
intuition
    in decision making, 142, 145
    developing, 60–61, 62

Johnson, Daniel, 10
Johnson, Peter, 10
journaling, 35
Juday, Dave, 31, 85–87, 116
Juday, Meghan, 86, 116

King Within, The: Accessing the King in the Male Psyche (Moore and Gillette), 77
Kobrand Corporation, 85
Kolocek, Lena, 86
Kopf, Rudy, 85

Label Makers Inc., 63, 105, 129
Lansberg, Ivan, 93, 114, 115, 140
leaders. *See also* successors
    authenticity of, 43, 44
    blind spots of, 46
    as change agents, 148
    characteristics of, 54, 98, 124–125, 162, 163
    credibility of. *See* credibility
    decision making by, 138–151

leaders *(continued)*
 differentiated, 9, 26, 29–30, 92,
   123–124, 131, 134, 151
 emotional intelligence of, 69,
   106
 failure as learning experience
   for, 64–68, 97, 144
 followers developed by, 49, 127,
   134
 generative approach of, 7, 76–78,
   84, 85, 133
 goal setting by, 95, 97, 100, 155
 insecurity in, 132–133, 150–151
 intuition of, 60–61
 motivations of, 96, 123, 127, 161
 perfectionism in, 143–144
 preparation for, 13, 14, 51
 priorities of, 175
 relationship with employees,
   125–126, 128–130, 132
 replacing, 84
 responsibility assumed by, 49–50
 sense of identity of, 5, 31–32,
   34–35
 shared power among, 114
 skills of, 6
 style of, 21, 42, 167
 types of, 81
 values of, 39, 52, 60
 vision of, 76, 100, 126–127, 132,
   154
Level 5 leadership, 130
life cycle
 continual learning from, 92–93
 and family stability, 149
 and generative leadership, 27
 overview of, 23–25
 successor evaluation of, 44
Lindow, Corinna, 173
Linwood Mining and Minerals
   Corporation, 153, 161

LMI Packaging Solutions, 63, 94,
   103, 104, 105, 116, 117, 123,
   145–146, 149
Loyola University Chicago, 24

Managing for the Long Run (Miller
   and Lebreton-Miller), 108
mastery, as employee motivation,
   130
McCarthy-Bush Corporation, 161,
   163
McKee, Mike, 116
meditation/mindfulness, 35
mentors, 37, 63, 65
Metricom, 59
mission
 community reach of, 128
 as constant, 162
 and decision making, 144
 for each generation, 83–84, 96
 function of, 78, 160–161
 identifying, 168
 personal, 154
 statement of, 94
money. *See also* wealth
 as business focus, 113–114, 128,
   133
 distribution of, 126
 function of, 130
Moran, Jean, 63–65, 67, 91, 93, 96,
   103–107, 116–118, 123, 142,
   145–146, 160
Moran, JP, 117
mortality
 of leaders, 151
 of parents, 29
motivation
 of employees, 129–130, 132
 of leaders, 96, 123, 127
Murphy's law, 64
myths. *See* family mythologies

narcissism, 9, 131
Nestlé, 71, 165
next generation. *See also* successors
    entitlement felt by, 55–56
    family support for, 161
    names shared by, 17
    negative impact of family myth
        on, 4–6, 155, 156
    positive impact of family myth
        on, 3–4
Next Generation Leadership
    Institute, 24, 79, 158, 167,
    173

OODA (observe, orient, decide,
    and act) loop, 147–148
orientation lock, 148, 149,
    150
"Overprotected Kid, The" (Rosin),
    68

Panera Bread, 60
parentification, 13
parents
    absence of, 8, 15
    children's pleasing of, 9–11, 31,
        96
    idealization by, 11–13, 45–46,
        142–143
    idealization of, 7–8, 28
    mortality of, 29
    myths encouraged by, 8–9
    reactions to children's failure,
        65–68
    responsibility taught by, 50, 56,
        68–69
    values transmitted by, 79
Peredis, Theodore, 86
performance
    standards for, 119
    of successor, 143

Perrino, Joe, 19–22, 25, 26–27, 31,
    33, 37, 38, 39, 66, 80–81, 84,
    151, 165
Perrino, Nick, 19–22, 25, 39, 66,
    80–81, 151
personality inventories, 34
Peterson, Jr., Bill, 15
Peterson, Sharon, 15
Peterson, Sr., Bill, 14–15
Peterson Construction, 14
Pieper, Torsten, 173
Pink, Daniel, 129–130
Playboy Enterprises, 41–44, 54, 127,
    134
Playboy magazine, 42, 43–44
power
    and authenticity, 45
    and leadership, 134
    and objective feedback, 48
professional networks, 63
profitability, and decision making,
    150

rebellion, vs. differentiation, 28
Reed, Christie, 165
reflection techniques, 34–35
resilience
    building, 49–51
    of companies, 137
    within families, 116–117
reskilling, 147
risk
    and decision making, 141
    as learning experience, 65, 66, 68
    motivation for taking, 78

self-awareness
    and credibility, 43, 123
    cultivating, 33–37, 91
    and failure, 67–68
    and intuitive decision making, 61

self-confidence
  building, 67, 68, 95
  and decision making, 139, 142,
    144
  defined, 99
  of generative leaders, 77
self-control, 98–99, 101
self-esteem
  and career choice, 80
  factors in, 12
  and failure, 65, 143, 156
  increasing, 43, 68
self-improvement, continual,
    89–101
small businesses, employee motiva-
    tion in, 129
stakeholders/shareholders
  and decision making, 150
  earning confidence of, 93
  family members as, 108–110, 115
  financial concerns of, 114
Standard & Poor's (S&P) 500, 107
Starwood Hotel Group, 75
Steinbrenner, George, 6
storytelling. *See also* heroic stories
  and differentiation, 61, 131
  emotion-driven, 99–100
  as instruction, 28
  about leadership, 76
  and personal responsibility, 49
strategic plans, 154–156, 157,
    158–159, 162, 163
Strauss, Anselm, 173
success
  defining, 31, 34, 62, 94–95
  false versions of, 9
  motivation for, 96
  past vs. future, 27, 95
succession plan, 51, 57, 83, 84
succession process
  conflict in, 22, 29–30
  and leader credibility, 93
  natural progression of, 32

successors. *See also* leaders
  accountability of, 48, 56, 69,
    143
  action plan for, 31, 62, 158,
    161–162, 167
  authenticity of, 22, 26, 29, 44,
    158
  commitment to family business,
    62–63, 80
  competition among, 113–114
  credibility of. *See* credibility
  decision making by, 51, 141,
    142
  differentiation by, 9–11, 22,
    25–27, 39, 61, 92, 123–124
  entitlement felt by, 12, 15, 30, 53,
    55–56
  failure as learning experience
    for, 64–68, 144
  family relationships of, 94,
    104–105, 115
  idealization of, 11–13, 142–143
  ideals developed by, 122
  identity search of, 5, 26, 29, 30,
    32–33, 38, 46, 63
  infantilization of, 13–14
  insecurity in, 132–133
  mission of, 168
  and myth deconstruction, 28–29,
    97
  names given to, 17
  negative impact of family myths
    on, 5, 32–33, 97
  outside work experience for,
    9–10, 63, 71, 85
  parentification of, 13
  positive impact of family myths
    on, 3
  predecessor conflict with, 22
  priorities set by, 176
  self-awareness of, 33, 37, 123
  siblings of, 105, 106, 149, 163
  skill sets of, 10, 163–164

as stewards of family legacy, 7,
16, 29, 34, 39, 54, 61, 78, 84,
94–95, 101, 105, 134, 155, 156,
157
strategic plans of, 154–156, 157,
158–159, 162
successful, 7, 16, 54, 93, 106, 108
values of, 79–80, 168
vision of, 78–79, 127, 131,
168–169
vulnerability of, 97, 99–100, 144
work as learning experience for,
50–51, 52–53
successor's curse, 25–27
Sykes, Chester, 63, 64, 65, 67, 105,
117, 129

Taittinger, Clovis, 83
Taittinger, Francois, 85
Taittinger, Jean, 74
Taittinger, Pierre Emmanuel,
73–76, 83, 84, 85, 160
Taittinger, Vitalie, 83
Taittinger Champagne, 73–76, 85
team building, 97
technology, impact of changes in,
135–137, 148
Tengelmann Group, 4, 17, 71
termination
of family member, 103, 106,
118–119, 140, 149
as leadership responsibility, 60
as learning experience, 59, 122
"Tests of a Prince, The"
(Lansberg), 93, 140
therapy, 35, 37
360-degree reviews, 34
Thurmond, Kathleen, 46–47
Tommy Boy (movie), 12
Trek Bicycle Corporation, 50, 53,
54
trust-fund babies, 55
tyrant behavior, 26

Tyson, John, 37–38, 49–50, 52, 77,
121–122, 124, 130, 145, 148
Tyson Foods, Inc., 37–38, 49, 52,
121–122

US Treasury, 139

values
business vs. personal, 37, 61,
74–76, 79, 80–83, 127–128,
154
decisions informed by, 141, 144
employee representation of, 131
and family focus, 116
flexibility of, 162
formed by successors, 27, 39, 52
function of, 78, 85, 94, 98, 140,
164
identifying, 168
learned through experience, 60
Old World vs. New World, 21
parent-instilled, 28
in strategic plan, 159–160
and successor differentiation,
30
transmitted by myth, 3, 4
vanity press, 5
Vermeer, Bob, 28, 67
Vermeer, Gary, 4
Vermeer Corporation, 4, 28, 67,
125
victimization, 15, 49, 99, 100–101,
133
vision
and decision making, 144, 150
in family businesses, 82, 84,
86–87
flexibility of, 162
function of, 78, 94, 140
identifying, 168–169
of leaders, 76, 100, 126–127, 132,
154
of successors, 96

Vistage, 65, 167
vocation, finding, 9–10, 25, 29, 33

Walsh, Froma, 116–117
wealth
　and accountability, 69
　driver of, 109
　vs. financial assets, 128
　and successor entitlement, 56
Winpak Portion Packaging, 145–146

work
　as learning experience, 50–51, 52–53
　outside family business, 9–10, 63, 71, 85
Wrigley, Jr., William (Bill), 5, 17, 37, 38, 51, 76, 84, 118, 126, 154–155, 157, 159, 160, 162
Wrigley, Sr., William (Bill), 159
Wrigley Company, 5, 154, 160, 162

YPO, 167